FINANCIAL FAITHFULNESS

FINANCIAL FAITHFULNESS

*Unlocking Scripture to Avoid
the Distraction of Money*

ROGER GUM

WITH MISSY SCHRADER

WESTBOW
PRESS
A DIVISION OF THOMAS NELSON

WestBow Press books may be ordered through booksellers or by contacting:

WestBow Press
A Division of Thomas Nelson
1663 Liberty Drive
Bloomington, IN 47403
www.westbowpress.com
1 (866) 928-1240

Names and minor details may have been changed in the real-life stories shared in this book to protect the privacy of the individuals mentioned.

ISBN: 978-1-4908-1537-4 (sc)
ISBN: 978-1-4908-1538-1 (hc)
ISBN: 978-1-4908-1536-7 (e)

Library of Congress Control Number: 2013920600

Printed in the United States of America.

WestBow Press rev. date: 11/08/2013

To my dear wife, Susan, and my wonderful boys, Griffin, Xander, and Keaton. Thanks for your unending support and for helping me focus on what matters most. Keep pursuing God with all your heart, soul, and mind.

CONTENTS

PREFACE

I n some respects, this book has been twenty-four years in the making. I graduated from the University of Kentucky in 1989 with a journalism/advertising degree. I also played baseball for the Wildcats.

I remember being at my second-base position in Athens, Georgia, when my classmates were walking across the stage in Lexington for graduation. Susan and I were getting married in three months, and I did not have a job yet. Between the fifty-four-game baseball schedule and the twenty-one hours I was taking during my final semester in order to graduate, I had no time to interview.

As I began to explore opportunities in the advertising world, it became apparent I would need to move to a big city, like Chicago or San Francisco, to acquire the most attractive job. That was not something Susan and I wanted to do. So I took an advertising sales job with the local CBS television affiliate in Lexington. While I thoroughly enjoyed my major in college, it took all of three months in the real world to figure out a career in advertising was not for me.

It was time to do the interview process in earnest, like I should have done during my last year in college. The process proved fruitful, and I landed a great sales job with a Fortune 500 company in Atlanta. Susan and I enjoyed the fast pace of a big southern city, and I gained valuable training and experience. We got established in a wonderful church and made lifelong friends in a Bible study group made up of young married couples.

After three years of working and growing in my faith, I began to question how I could best use my gifts and skills in a vocation to glorify God. While I respected the family values of the company I worked for, I ultimately longed to do something more significant with my career.

A few years earlier, someone had given me some simple advice about choosing a job. They encouraged me to find people who seemed to enjoy their work and who did something I would want to do. As I reflected on this advice, I immediately thought of Chris, one of my friends in our small Bible study group. I began to pepper Chris, a financial planner, with questions about his job. The more he talked, the more excited I became. I realized that whenever I had time to read, I almost always gravitated to financial books and magazines.

I asked Chris what I needed to do to begin a career in financial planning. Knowing my major was not exactly conducive to this move, he suggested that I enroll in the Certified Financial Planner™ program. This was a two-year course that would indicate to prospective employers that I was serious about the field. It would also provide me with valuable foundational knowledge. I began the CFP® program, and I loved it.

As my desire to become a financial planner grew, I spent time researching the industry. Around this same time, our church began to require leaders of a small-group Bible study to meet with an elder for accountability. It turned out that my elder (Hunter) was a financial advisor!

Hunter worked for Ronald Blue & Co. As he learned of my interest in financial planning, he invited me to lunch and took me on a tour of the Atlanta headquarters. As soon as I saw the firm's mission—"Ronald Blue & Co. exists to help Christians become financially free to assist in fulfilling the Great Commission"—I was hooked. Combining biblical principles of finance with technical expertise was beyond compelling to me.

I went home that day and told Susan, "I don't know when and I don't know how, but one day I will work for Ronald Blue & Co." With my new excitement for financial planning, my enthusiasm for my current job began to wane.

After completing the first year of the CFP® course, my manager at my current job came to me with a tremendous opportunity. He offered me a significant promotion to the corporate headquarters to be part of the strategic planning team. This company only promoted from within its current employees, and this was one of the most desired positions. Still hoping to move into financial planning, I quickly sent out resumes to several firms to see if anyone was interested in hiring me. They all came back with the same response: "Talk to us when you complete your CFP® course."

Susan and I continued to pray, asking God for direction. While I felt that I would eventually make a career change into financial planning, it could be years before that would occur. While this promotion was a great opportunity that would provide me with wonderful experience, the corporate headquarters were in St. Paul, Minnesota. We had just had our first son, Griffin, and we would be a long plane ride away from family and friends. After much prayer and discussion, we decided to embark on an adventure and go to St. Paul.

We moved the week before Thanksgiving to Minnesota, which might as well have been a foreign country. We did not know how to dress, how to talk, or how to handle the winter. In short, nothing seemed to go right. We were lonely, Griffin was constantly sick, and life seemed to revolve around the weather. To make matters worse for Susan, my job was extremely demanding, and the hours at the office were very long.

Three months into our move, we were seriously questioning our decision. Had we just missed God's plan for us? Should we have stayed in Atlanta? This questioning process matched an intense two weeks of bitter temperatures that never rose above zero degrees! We had come to St. Paul with tennis shoes and windbreakers, unprepared for the battle with the weather.

In the midst of this cold snap, I received a phone call one Sunday afternoon from my Atlanta friend Chris. He asked, "Are you still interested in financial planning?"

"More than ever," I replied.

He told me Hunter was opening up a RB&Co. branch office in Charlotte and was looking for a financial planner. Chris suggested I give him a call.

I thanked Chris and immediately called Hunter's home in Atlanta. His wife answered the phone and told me Hunter was pulling out of the driveway to go to Charlotte, where he was preparing to open the office the next day. She ran outside and flagged him down. Hunter and I talked for about forty-five minutes. There seemed to be an immediate synergy between us. Hunter was interested in considering me for his open planner position, and I was elated!

The interview process continued for several months. While I did not have the ideal experience or education background, my progress through the CFP® course was important, and it seemed Hunter and I would work very well together. In addition, what I was learning at my current company's corporate headquarters in Minnesota was significant.

Six months after moving to Minnesota, I was offered the job of financial planner in the Charlotte office of Ronald Blue & Co. On April 30, 1994, Susan and I left winter in St. Paul, drove through spring somewhere in Kentucky, and arrived in summer in Charlotte, North Carolina. We were thrilled to be hot!

God had graciously answered our prayers. He allowed me to work for a company whose mission was irresistible. From the moment I began at RB&Co., I had a deep passion for biblical principles of finance. I read everything I could that had to do with handling money from a biblical perspective. And I began the joyful journey of helping individuals become faithful stewards.

Four years into my career at RB&Co., I was asked to teach a twelve-week Sunday school series at my church on biblical principles of finance. I titled the course "Putting Your Financial House in Order." After teaching this curriculum several times, someone mentioned I should publish the material. It took me fifteen years and many revisions, but I was finally able to publish it!

ACKNOWLEDGMENTS

I am so thankful for the many people who have contributed to this book through their help, insight, and teaching.

This book would not have been possible without the support and encouragement of my wonderful wife, Susan. Throughout these pages, I share what we have been learning together for twenty-four amazing years of marriage. She is the love of my life, and her life is a constant example of loving God and loving others well.

It is a privilege to be the father of Griffin, Xander, and Keaton. God has taught me many powerful lessons through their lives. I love each of them dearly.

While I have toyed with writing this book for over fifteen years, it did not become a reality until Missy Schrader agreed to walk alongside me. I am so thankful for her tremendous skill and inspiration in helping me to scrub and edit my raw material until it finally became presentable.

I am grateful for the wise teachings and writings of Dr. Wayne Poplin, Andy Stanley, Randy Alcorn, and Alex Kennedy. God has used each of them to unlock the power and application of Scripture in my life.

I am forever appreciative to my parents, Roger W. Gum II and Louise Gum, who provided a wonderful foundation for me, instilling in me the priority of loving and serving God.

To my team members at Ronald Blue & Co., I am thankful for their patience, as I am sure they often wondered, *Will this book ever be done?* I appreciate the passion with which they each do their jobs, and for the love and care they show our clients. It is a pleasure to co-labor with them.

INTRODUCTION

O ne of the great challenges of life is to limit distractions in order to focus on what matters the most. Regardless of how much or how little we have, issues of money threaten to sidetrack us.

If we have a lot of money, we fear losing what we possess. We are tempted to put our hope in our wealth instead of God. If we don't have so much, we stress about not having enough to provide for our families and are often consumed with the desire for more.

The most important aspect of my job as a financial planner is helping people see money from a biblical perspective. If we are able to achieve this, the diversion of money will be much less of an issue in our lives.

Let me tell you a true story to explain how powerful perspective can be.

Airplane Man

A few years ago, my friend Wayne tore his ACL while playing pickup basketball. The injury required surgery.

Immediately after the operation, he began rehabilitation at the University of Virginia. He had to wake up to the bitter cold at

5:00 a.m., ice his knee, struggle to get ready while maneuvering on his crutches, and drive for an hour to make his appointment.

Physical therapy was strenuous and painful. One machine he especially hated was nicknamed "the Beast." This mass of metal, bars, and weights inflicted pain like he had never experienced. Before long, he began to dread his early morning routine and became increasingly frustrated with the circumstances of his injury.

One morning after finishing his battle with the Beast, Wayne saw someone coming through the door who caught his attention. This man was in a cast from his waist to his neck. His arms were connected to his waist by wires that kept him outstretched like a child pretending to be an airplane. He had to turn sideways just to fit through the door. The immobilized patient only stayed in the room for a few minutes before being escorted to another section of the building.

Partly out of curiosity and partly out of wanting to delay his next encounter with the Beast, Wayne asked the nurse who had assisted the man what happened to him. She said he fell out of a second-story window and broke almost every bone in his back and upper body. He would be in the cast that covered his entire torso for months, and he was dealing with severe pain.[1]

As Wayne returned to his physical therapy regimen, he had renewed energy. After seeing the "airplane man," his situation did not seem so bad.

When the alarm rang at 5:00 a.m. the next day, Wayne was not as tired as usual. When he went outside, the cold air did not feel as biting, and the drive to UVA did not seem as long. He had so much motivation during his workout that he even did an extra set of reps on the Beast!

In reality, Wayne's circumstances had not changed at all. The weather report said it was just as cold as the day before. He drove the same number of miles. And the pain from his workout was still intense. Everything was the same, but he felt different, very different.

Why?

His perspective had changed, and that changed everything.

The goal of Financial Faithfulness is to challenge our perspective concerning money. Having a biblical mentality will not change our financial circumstances, at least not right away. But just like seeing the "airplane man" changed Wayne's mindset, I pray the principles we explore in this book will transform our financial outlook.

As we begin to see money from a biblical perspective, we will be well on our way to the financial freedom and peace of mind that everyone desires but few find.

CHAPTER 1

WHY A BIBLICAL PERSPECTIVE?

"**M**ine! Mine!" shouts a toddler who does not want to share his toys. A twelve-year-old's Christmas list includes a cell phone and an iPad. A teenager expects a new car for her sixteenth birthday. A young wife is thrilled with her first home, until she visits her friend's professionally decorated house. A husband envies his friend's boat and impulsively buys one of his own. The toys are all different, but the underlying issue is the same: it is easy to believe more money and more stuff will make us happy.

Why is it important to discover what God says about money in the Bible? Let's look at four compelling reasons.

Money Talks

God talks about money a lot, a whole lot. In fact, there are over 2,350 verses in the Bible that reference money—more than on faith and prayer combined. Scripture says more about money than it does about heaven and hell. Fifteen percent of Christ's words and two-thirds of His parables are devoted to the topic of money.[2]

Why does the Bible have so much to say about money? All those verses about money are not simply about money. They teach us about God and His character, our own heart, the nature of sin, and about loving others. God's frequent use of money in Scripture indicates the topic is important to Him. So as believers, cultivating a biblical perspective on finances should be critical to us, too. As we will see, a significant connection exists between our spiritual lives and how we handle money.

A Mark of Maturity

As believers, we know our fundamental purpose in life is to glorify God. One of the ways we extol our Creator is by being obedient and holy. How we deal with money is an indicator of where we are in this process of sanctification. In Scripture, the proof of true spiritual change is often related to a radical change in our behavior toward our possessions. Consider Acts 2:44–45 (NASB).

> And all those who had believed were together and had all things in common; and they began selling their property and possessions, and were sharing them with all, as anyone might have need.

The Christians in this first church were certainly much more generous with their possessions after they believed in Jesus. Their behaviors, including how they handled money, completely changed with conversion. These young believers are great examples for us when we struggle to incorporate our beliefs into our conduct.

George Barna, the well-known researcher of faith and culture, says, "Millions of people who rely on Jesus Christ for their eternal destiny have problems translating their religious beliefs into action beyond Sunday mornings."[3] This difficulty of faith application is especially evident when it comes to money, as Christians often look like the rest of the world financially. As Christ-followers who desire to glorify God, we show our movement toward spiritual maturity in part by the way we treat our wealth.

We Are Hit Hard

Will we have a worldly perspective of riches or a biblical one? We are constantly bombarded with our culture's claims that we can find security, happiness, and fulfillment through riches. Movies, advertisements, social media, and television shows relentlessly proclaim contentment is found when there is an abundance of wealth.

To offset these materialistic influences, we should immerse ourselves in the Bible, studying its principles about money. Otherwise, the sheer volume of what we hear and see will overwhelm us and seep into our beliefs and behaviors.

In Philippians 4:11–12 (NIV), Paul says, "for I have learned to be content whatever the circumstances. I know what it is to be in need, and I know what it is to have plenty. I have learned the secret of being content in any and every situation, whether well fed or hungry, whether living in plenty or in want."

The world's falsehoods concerning what will make us content are easy to believe. Yet Paul uses the word "learned" to assure us that viewing money and possessions from a scriptural mind-set is a process that can be achieved. The beauty of the contentment Paul describes results from understanding money and life from God's perspective.

Beware of Danger

There is a lot of money in this world. This may not sound like a problem, but wealth can be extremely dangerous.

And Jesus said to His disciples, "Truly I say to
you, it is hard for a rich man to enter the kingdom
of heaven. Again I say to you, it is easier for a
camel to go through the eye of a needle, than for
a rich man to enter the kingdom of God." When
the disciples heard this, they were astonished
and said, "Then who then can be saved?" (Matt.
19:23–25 NASB)

Why does Jesus single out the rich? He knows our temptation
to love money is greater when we have a lot of it. Jesus was not
saying the rich cannot go to heaven. He was saying that wealth
tempts us to put our hopes in money rather than in God. It is
essential to have our eyes wide open to the possible perils of
money, especially if we are rich.

So who are the rich? Several years ago Fidelity Investments
hired Northstar Research Partners to survey over one thousand
households with average investable assets of $3.5 million. Almost
42 percent said they did not feel wealthy, stating they would need
$7.5 million to feel rich.[4] The Global Rich List, however, points out
that anyone who makes $47,500 or more in a year ranks in the top
1 percent of the world's income.[5]

In his book Money, Possessions and Eternity, Randy Alcorn
writes,

If you have sufficient food, decent clothes, live in
a house that keeps the weather out, and own a
reasonably reliable means of transportation, you
are among the top 15 percent of the world's wealthy.
If you have any money saved, a hobby that requires
some equipment or supplies, a variety of clothes in
your closet, two cars, and live in your own home,
you are in the top 5 percent of the world's wealthy.[6]

So who are the rich? You and me. Society admires and encourages financial accumulation. But beware, this pursuit can be dangerous.

> For the love of money is a root of all sorts of evil, and some by longing for it have wandered away from the faith and pierced themselves with many griefs. (1 Tim. 6:10 NASB)

Scripture warns us of the hazards that lurk with money, especially with a lot of it. A biblical perspective is critical to safeguarding against these pitfalls.

What Is a Biblical Perspective of Money?

Let's examine four ways we can begin to think biblically about our finances.

It's All His

God owns it all. We are simply called to be faithful stewards of what belongs to Him.

> A steward is someone entrusted with another's wealth or property and charged with the responsibility of managing it in the owner's best interest.[7]

And what is required of a steward? First Corinthians 4:2 (ESV) tells us, "Moreover, it is required of stewards that they be found trustworthy."

What does it mean to be found trustworthy or faithful? About thirteen years ago, my two oldest sons, Griffin and Xander, played soccer in a six and under league. The kids played four-on-four, including the goalie. At four years old, Xander was the youngest player in the league (I had to talk the commissioner into letting him play), and Griffin was one of the oldest.

They both had a great time. But as you can imagine, Griffin enjoyed a lot of success, while Xander did not. In fact, going into the last game of the year, Xander and another player, Blair, were the only ones on the team who had not scored a goal.

During the last quarter of the last game, the coach put Xander and Blair in the game with specific instructions to stay by the opponent's goal. Then he ordered Griffin to stop the other team by himself, and to feed passes to Xander and Blair to help them score.

As the quarter began, Griffin chased the other team's players downfield, stole the ball, and kicked a perfect pass toward the goal, only to find both of his teammates had wandered off to the woods, where they had seen a squirrel. Coach called the only timeout of the season and placed the two non-scorers on the line, six feet from the opponent's goal, and said, "Don't leave this line!"

As play continued, Griffin gained control of the ball and fed a pass toward Xander and Blair. But the pass came up a few feet short of the goalie box line. Xander and Blair, remembering their coach's instructions to stay on the line, stretched as far as they could but were not able to reach the ball.

By this time, all the parents from both sides were cheering for the two to score. Griffin kicked another pass in the air to Xander who, thinking the ball was going to hit him in the head, ducked out of the way. For the entire ten-minute quarter, Griffin exhausted himself blocking, stealing, and passing. And while the other team did not score, neither did Xander nor Blair.

The game ended, and the season was over. All the parents clapped. Xander and Blair came running off the field happily. Everyone was cheering.

Then I glanced down to the other end of the field and saw Griffin coming toward me. He was clearly upset. With tears streaming down his face, he said, "Dad, I did everything I could, but they didn't score!"

And he absolutely had done everything he could do. In one of those rare moments when God gave me just the right words to say, I gave him a big hug and said, "Griffin, you *did* do everything you could do. You did what the coach asked you to do, and I am so proud of you!"

You see, Griffin was faithful, even though Xander and Blair did not score. His faithfulness had nothing to do with the final result. He did what he was instructed to do, and that made him trustworthy.

At that moment, I realized this is what God requires of us in order to be faithful. Faithfulness is about pleasing our Master! And we please Him through obedience. God is in charge of the results.

Contentment in Him

We must learn that money does not equal contentment.

> But godliness actually is a means of great gain, when accompanied by contentment. For we have brought nothing into the world, so we cannot take anything out of it either. And if we have food and covering, with these we shall be content. (1 Tim. 6:6–8 NASB)

Paul says that beyond food and covering, money should have nothing to do with our contentment. That's hard, isn't it? Most of us have food, clothing, and a roof over our heads, but we are not always content. We live in a world that defines contentment with one word ... more!

Read what John Steinbeck said to Adlai Stevenson in a letter printed in the Washington Post on January 28, 1960: "A strange species we are. We can stand anything God and nature can throw at us save only plenty. If I wanted to destroy a nation, I would give it too much, and I would have it on its knees, miserable, greedy, sick."[8]

Money does not provide contentment, and the richest of the rich in our society prove it. Psychologist and social scientist Dacher Keltner says, "The rich really are different, but not in a good way: Their life experience makes them less empathetic, less altruistic, and generally more selfish."[9]

Richard Watts knows more about the wealthy than most. He provides legal counsel to the super-rich, families with $100 million or more. Surely if money brings contentment, these people would know it. In his book Fables of Fortune: What Rich People Have That You Don't Want, Watts says, "They [the rich] feed at the table of materialism without ever being satisfied."[10]

The world's myth that money and possessions guarantee contentment is simply false. If it were true, those who have the least would be the most dissatisfied. Yet the most content Christians I've ever met have almost no material possessions at all.

I travel to the Dominican Republic (DR) every year to do mission work. The DR is wonderful country, but it is a poor country, and we do much of our ministry in poverty-stricken sugarcane villages. The believers we meet have almost nothing, but they are more content than many Americans.

Don't get me wrong; they have needs. But they are content. On a recent trip, we saw kids playing baseball with a papaya and a small tree limb. We offered them a baseball. They looked at it, threw it to the side, and continued their game with the papaya!

I have taken my boys with me on several of these trips. Each one has asked me the same question: "Dad, how can they be so happy when they don't have anything?" These Dominican Christians realize true contentment and joy comes from who they are in Christ and from the hope He has given them.

They are not tempted to find satisfaction in money or in things. They rarely, if ever, see any images of wealth. They don't dream of mansions and fancy cars; they dream of heaven. And yet, even after visiting seven times, the desire to give these believers more things still overcomes me. Why? Because I struggle with this notion that money and stuff bring satisfaction. In reality, the Dominican Christians are teaching me about true contentment!

Watch Your Desires

> But those who want to get rich fall into temptation and a snare and many foolish and harmful desires which plunge men into ruin and destruction. (1 Tim. 6:9 NASB)

It is very tempting to become consumed with acquiring money and things, because being rich in our society is associated with luxury, pleasure, and a carefree life.

> It is a very serious thing to grow rich. Of all the temptations to which God's children are exposed, it is the worst, because it is the one they do not dread. Therefore, it is the more subtle temptation.[11] (Charles Haddon Spurgeon)

A specific amount of money is not the problem. The trouble is the pursuit and love of money, which never delivers the satisfaction it promises. As believers, our heart's desire must be to pursue and love Christ, who always satisfies.

God Is Our Hope

> Instruct those who are rich in this present world not to be conceited or to fix their hope on the uncertainty of riches, but on God, who richly supplies us with all things to enjoy. (1 Tim. 6:17 NASB)

Remember, we are all rich, so this verse is for us. Listen carefully to the warning. It doesn't say we should be poor. It says we should fix our hope on God, even when we are wealthy.

The uncertainty of wealth was made painfully clear during the stock market crash of 2008 and 2009. On October 9, 2007, the Dow Jones Industrial Average (DJIA) closed at a record high of 14,164.53. Over the next seventeen months, there was an intense downturn. The severe financial crises brought the DJIA to a closing low of 6,547.05 on March 9, 2009, which represented a drop of almost 54 percent. During just eight trading days in October 2008, the index shrunk by 22.1 percent!

This catastrophic decline proved the unpredictability of wealth. The days following the crash were significant. Why? Because the truth of Scripture was put to the test. When wealth is taken away, it becomes clear whether our security is in our riches or in God. Our reaction to loss is revealing.

My sleep, my mood, my outlook, and my relationships were all negatively affected by this loss of wealth. I had to confess that my hope was on riches rather than on God. It was when I was faced with wealth's uncertainty that I experienced what it really means to put my hope in God.

Here We Go!

The goal of *Financial Faithfulness* is to help Christ-followers develop a Christ-centered view of money. But we are not going to stop there. We want this mind-set to translate into our behavior. To do that, we will learn how to practically apply a biblical perspective into our everyday dealings with money.

CHAPTER 2

THE PURPOSE OF MONEY

In order to develop a biblical perspective of wealth, we need to begin with a correct understanding of money. To do this, let's first examine what money is not. Then we'll look at what money is.

What Money Is Not

Money Is Not a Measure of Our Worth

It is very natural to use money as a gauge of a person's worth. Most of us do this without even thinking about it. When someone meets another person for the first time, what is the typical first question? "What do you do?"

We make judgments based on the prestige and income associated with his answer. Not only do we make conclusions about others based on their work and income, we do the same about ourselves. Scripture proclaims that who we are is much more than our vocation or net worth.

For by grace you have been saved through faith;
and that not of yourselves, it is the gift of God; not
as a result of works, that no one should boast. For
we are His workmanship, created in Christ Jesus
for good works, which God prepared beforehand,
that we should walk in them. (Eph. 2:8–10 NASB)

We are His workmanship! A bounty of possessions does
not equal value; yet we often live as if it does. Let's look at a
story from the gospel of Luke to remind us of our significance
in Christ.

During biblical times, the Jewish custom required the oldest
son to receive twice the inheritance of any other sons. Luke tells of
two Jewish brothers, whose parents had recently died. Consistent
with the tradition, the older son received a double bequest. His
brother was outraged.

On hearing that a wise, all-knowing rabbi—Jesus—was
visiting their town, the younger son made a plan to go see this
teacher, hoping He would correct this injustice by requiring
equality. Fighting through the crowd, the sibling found Jesus
and begged, "Teacher, Rabbi, tell my brother to give me what is
rightfully mine."

Knowing this young man believed having more money
would improve his life, Jesus responded, "Beware, and be on
your guard against every form of greed; for not even when one
has an abundance does his life consist of his possessions" (Luke
12:15 NASB).

Later, in John, Jesus reminds us where we can find abundant
life: I came that they may have life, and have it abundantly (John
10:10b NASB).

Our true worth is not our net worth. Our value completely
depends on what Jesus did for us by dying on the cross to forgive
our sins.

Money Is Not a Reward for Godly Living

Scripture is full of both rich and poor who experienced God's favor. If money were a reward for godly living, men like Paul would certainly have been among the wealthiest. But he lost all things for Christ's sake and considered his poverty a blessing, desiring nothing more than knowing Christ (Phil. 3:7–10).

Randy Alcorn shares this powerful anecdote to further drive this point home.

> In California, a sharp-looking businessman stands up at a luncheon to give his testimony: "before I knew Christ, I had nothing. My business was in bankruptcy, my health was ruined, I'd lost the respect of the community, and I'd almost lost my family. Then I accepted Christ as my Savior and Lord. He took me out of bankruptcy and now my business has tripled its profits in the last three years. My blood pressure has dropped to normal, and I feel better than I've felt in years. And, best of all, my wife and children have come back, and we're a family again. God is good—Praise the Lord!"

> In China, an old and disheveled former university professor gives his testimony: "Before I met Christ, I had everything. I made a large salary, lived in a nice house, enjoyed good health, was highly respected for my credentials and profession, and had a good marriage and beautiful children. Then I accepted Christ as my Savior and Lord. As a result, I lost my post at the university, lost my beautiful house and car, and spent five years in prison. Now I work for a subsistence wage at a factory, and I live

in pain from my neck that was broken in prison. My wife rejected me because of my conversion. She took my children away and I haven't seen her or them for ten years. But God is good, and I praise Him for His faithfulness."

Both men are sincere Christians. One gives thanks because of what he has gained. The other gives thanks in spite of what he has lost.[12]

Christ does not promise financial riches in exchange for an obedient life. God's blessings are numerous, varied, and undeserved. Our heavenly Father's favor should never be measured based on financial standing.

Money Is Not a Measure of Success

Typically, we associate money with success. A "successful" businessperson makes profitable deals and acquires financial gain. A "successful" entrepreneur sells his or her business for a huge profit. Although we would consider these people to be affluent, Scripture says something different about true success.

> This book of the law shall not depart from your mouth, but you shall meditate on it day and night, so that you may be careful to do according to all that is written in it; for then you will make your way prosperous, and then you will have success. (Josh. 1:8 NASB)

While the world associates success with money and prestige, God defines success as knowing God's law and obeying what it says.

What Money Is

Money Is a Tool

A tool is something that helps us complete a task more efficiently and effectively. You can dig a ditch with your hands, but it is a lot easier with a shovel. Your goal is not to have the nicest shovel; it is simply to dig a ditch.

As believers, accumulating money is not worthy of our primary focus. Instead, our fundamental purpose is to glorify God and enjoy Him forever. When our ultimate objective is financial, it is like thinking you're finished after buying a shovel without ever digging a ditch!

How can money be used as a tool?

A Tool of Discipline

Since we all possess unlimited ways to spend limited resources, living within our means requires self-control. Yet according to the Homeownership Preservation Foundation, 43 percent of American families spend more than they make.[13] No matter how much a person earns, it is always possible to spend more.

I will never forget the cardiologist who came into my office for an initial meeting. He made $750,000 a year but was spending $800,000! He said if he could just earn $100,000 more each year, he knew he could make significant progress toward achieving his financial goals. Although he believed more money would solve his problems, the truth was he needed self-control. Money is a tool that teaches us discipline as we learn to be content with God's provision.

A Tool to Fulfill the Great Commission

We do not want to stand in the way of God's providential will— that which is going to happen no matter what we do or don't do. Pharaoh's failure to cooperate with God's plans left him at the bottom of the Red Sea (Ex. 14:28). Participating in God's purposes, such as fulfilling the Great Commission, results in eternal blessings. Matthew 24:14 says, "And this gospel of the kingdom will be preached in the whole world as a testimony to all nations, and then the end will come." Although God doesn't need us or our money to reach the world, He chooses to use both.

According to the Issachar Initiative, the coordinated efforts of multiple ministries, combined with the use of new technology and the donations of thousands, can lead to the fulfillment of the Great Commission in our generation![14] Here are two ministries working toward this purpose.

Almost two thousand languages still do not have a translation of the Bible. The mission of Wycliffe Bible Translators' Last Languages Campaign is to have either a written or oral Bible translation program started for every tongue by the year 2025.[15]

Using a combination of television, churches, and relationships, the Billy Graham Evangelistic Association presents the gospel message to an entire country. To date, the My Hope Project has reached fifty-seven countries with over ten million coming to faith in Jesus Christ![16]

Many ministries use donated money to reach the lost for Christ and to make disciples. What a magnificent privilege it is to use our money as a tool to carry out the Great Commission.

A Tool to Move Us toward Holiness

In Leviticus 19, God says, "Be holy because I, the Lord your God, am holy." Then, while giving Moses instructions for His people, God commands the Israelites to leave some gleanings for the poor as they harvest their fields. The Father's command to be holy is followed by an exhortation to share. God is boundlessly generous. In fact, the only verse in the Bible where we are told to test God has to do with His own bounty.

"Bring the whole tithe into the storehouse, so that there may be food in my house, and test Me now in this," says the LORD of hosts, "if I will not open for you the windows of heaven and pour out for you a blessing until it overflows." (Mal. 3:10 NIV)

We must decide whether our money is primarily for our comfort or if some of it is for others. When we are generous, we reflect our Father in heaven, who says much about sharing.

Give generously to them and do so without a grudging heart; (Deut. 15:10a NIV)

Instruct them to do good, to be rich in good works, to be generous and ready to share. (1 Tim. 6:18 NASB)

Give to everyone who asks of you, (Luke 6:30a NASB)

It is more blessed to give than to receive. (Acts 20:35b NASB)

When an ice cream sundae cost much less than it does today, a boy entered a coffee shop and sat at a table. A waitress put a glass of water in front of him.

"How much is an ice cream sundae?" he asked.

"Fifty cents," replied the waitress.

The little boy pulled his hand out of his pocket and studied a number of coins in it.

"How much is a dish of plain ice cream?" he inquired. Some people were now waiting for a table, and the waitress was becoming impatient.

"Thirty-five cents," she said angrily.

The little boy again counted the coins. "I'll just have the plain ice cream."

The waitress brought the ice cream and walked away. The boy finished, paid the thirty-five cents, and left the store. When the waitress returned to his empty table, she found a gift for her—two nickels and five pennies placed neatly beside his empty dish—her tip.[17]

This young boy knew the joy that comes from being generous. He chose a little less for himself so that he could be kind to the waitress. Money provides us the opportunity to reflect God's holiness.

Money Is a Test

The test money sets before us is multifaceted.

A Test of Our Loyalties

> No servant can serve two masters; for either he will hate the one and love the other, or else he will be devoted to one and despise the other. You cannot serve God and wealth. (Luke 16:13 NASB)

As a believer, money presents the ultimate test of our allegiance. We can only have one master; we are either wholeheartedly devoted to God or not at all.

Imagine an ambassador who represents his mother country while living in a foreign land. He learns about his new home by familiarizing himself with the people and the culture. As he spends more time in this alien nation, he begins to enjoy his new surroundings; his comfort increases, and his loyalty vacillates as he considers this new country to be better than his own. In doing so, he becomes ineffective in his primary responsibility of representing his homeland.[18]

The first commandment God gave Moses spoke to our heart's allegiance: "You shall not make for yourself an idol in the form of anything in heaven above or on the earth beneath or in the waters below." As Christians, we are Christ's servants, and our loyalty should be to Him alone. Like the ambassador who melted into the new culture, we betray our Father in heaven when money steals the affection reserved for God. The temptation to love money will constantly test our devotion to Him.

A Test of Our Perspective

> But store up for yourselves treasures in heaven, where neither moth nor rust destroys, and where thieves do not break in or steal; for where your treasure is, there will your heart be also. (Matt. 6:20, 21 NASB)

The things of this world tempt us to live for the temporal, but we are called to have an eternal perspective, focusing on what lasts forever—God's Word and the souls of men and women. In John Ortberg's book *When the Game Is Over, It All Goes Back in the Box*, he reminds us that our possessions are short-lived.[19] Seeing through eternal lenses allows us to hold money with open hands, since it all goes "back in the box" at the end of life's game.

> It is since Christians have largely ceased to think of the other world that they have become so ineffective in this one. (C. S. Lewis)

Money is a constant test of our perspective. Will it be temporal or eternal?

Money Is a Testimony

> You are the light of the world. A city set on a hill cannot be hidden; nor does anyone light a lamp, and put it under a basket, but on the lampstand, and it gives light to all who are in the house. Let your light shine before men in such a way that they may see your good works, and glorify your Father who is in heaven. (Matt. 5:14–16 NASB)

As Christians, we are called to live in a way that points others to Christ. The world's view of handling wealth is radically different from the one presented in the Bible. So we have an incredible opportunity to be a light unto the world with our money. I once heard Dr. Howard Hendricks speak when he asked this challenging question: "If you were accused of being a Christian, and the only evidence was your checkbook, would it be enough to convict you?"[20]

A friend recently shared with me that she received an unexpected call from her accountant. It was unusual, because she only talks to the accountant in April, and this call came in January. While she has used this tax preparer for several years, she does not know him personally. In the conversation, he shared that he had recently been diagnosed with cancer, and he wanted her to pray for him.

Why did he ask her?

He confided, "I have seen how you have spent your money over the years, and I knew that you would pray for me!"

Can you imagine the power of the collective testimonies of millions of believers managing money and possessions in accordance to the principles laid out in Scripture?

Take Heart

If having a biblical perspective of money seems overwhelming, take heart! As believers, we possess the power of the almighty God of hope and love, who promises to provide for our needs. He is on this journey with us! Pray this prayer with me as we continue.

> Lord, help me put on your eternal lenses. I want to
> see all I have as yours. I desire to be your faithful
> steward. In Jesus's name, Amen.

CHAPTER 3

MAKING WISE FINANCIAL DECISIONS

Imagine a sprinter preparing to run a 100-meter race. When the gun fires, all of the runners dash for the finish line except him. He runs hard but without direction, not knowing where the tape is. We can't imagine an athlete being so foolish. After all, the placement of the finish line determines everything about the race. Yet many of us run our financial lives without any idea of where our finish lines are. Lacking clearly defined goals, the years pass without the type of meaningful progress we desire because we don't know what we are trying to accomplish.

Goals Provide Direction and Purpose

If you aim at nothing, you will hit it every time. If you do not know where you are going, any road will get you there.

Without goals, our financial decisions are dictated by other people, unchecked emotions, and perceived urgency, all of which obstruct wise decision making.

And do not be conformed to this world, but be transformed by the renewing of your mind, so that you may prove what the will of God is, that which is good and acceptable and perfect. (Rom. 12:2 NASB)

Most of us are satisfied with simply accumulating as much as we can, which is the world's way of thinking. Since the longing for more is insatiable, we never experience financial freedom. When we choose to set financial objectives, our choices become purposeful, and we stay focused on what is most important. But just developing goals is not enough.

Write Them Down

According to a Dominican University study, those who write out their goals are much more likely to accomplish them than those who don't. The study concludes that for maximum achievement, one needs to write them down, share them with someone else, and be held accountable.[21]

When my oldest son, Griffin, was in the eighth grade, a coach at a sports camp he attended challenged the boys to write down their goals. Griffin took the message to heart and wrote down his objective on a 3 x 5 card that he taped to his bathroom mirror. "I will play in the MLB one day." He shared it with us, and we smiled and applauded his ambition.

Two years later, as a sophomore in high school, he began to see life a little more realistically. He amended his goal to, "I will play collegiate baseball one day." After shoulder surgery during his junior year, he added this phrase to the end, "if it's God's will."

It turned out that it was God's will, and Griffin went on to play college baseball in a wonderful program at the University of Alabama at Birmingham. Having that note on his mirror was a constant reminder to Griffin to work hard and stay focused.

I greatly respected how he recognized, though, that what he ultimately wanted was up to God's will.

The way Griffin set his target is a great example for us. In order to be intentional with our financial goals, write them down, share them with someone else, be held accountable, and surrender each goal to our heavenly Father—*if it is God's will.* "Commit your works to the Lord and your plans will be established (Prov. 16:3 NASB).

A sample agenda for a goal-setting weekend can be found at *www.FinFaith.com.* My clients who have completed this intentional weekend rave about its effectiveness in establishing financial unity, focus, and purpose.

Steps to Making Wise Financial Decisions

Once you've clearly written out your financial goals, you have a framework for making purposeful decisions in order to accomplish your objectives. But how do you make sure your decisions are wise?

Seek Biblical Wisdom

> Your word is a lamp to my feet and a light to my
> path. (Ps. 119:105 NASB)

The Bible is full of verses that provide us with wisdom for all decisions, even financial ones. As we explore in these remaining chapters, many of the answers to our financial questions are already laid out for us in Scripture.

Pray

> But if any of you lacks wisdom, let him ask of God,
> who gives to all generously and without reproach,
> and it will be given to him. (Jas. 1:5 NASB)

We need to pray about all our financial decisions—a home, a car, investments, job decisions, even buying a television. God makes His perfect wisdom available to us when we ask. Take advantage of His gracious offer!

Be in Agreement with Your Spouse

> I appeal to you, brothers and sisters, in the name of our Lord Jesus Christ, that all of you agree with one another in what you say and that there be no divisions among you, but that you be perfectly united in mind and thought. (1 Cor. 1:10 NIV)

What do you think is the number-one area of disagreements and arguments among married couples? You guessed it—money.[22] Nothing else comes close to winning that first-place spot.

God honors unity. Unfortunately, many couples don't experience financial harmony. Over the years, I have seen many bad financial decisions that could have been avoided if husbands and wives committed to agree before proceeding.

There are no grounds for the "I told you so" response if we practice the principle of unity. Just as important, I have seen some good financial decisions that ended up being detrimental to a marriage, because one spouse didn't consult the other. The result of the decision never justifies the lack of unity.

Do not ignore the advice and counsel of your spouse. Even when one spouse may not understand as much as the other about financial matters, it is still critical to be of the same mind before making significant financial decisions. A friend defines this as any purchase of $100 or more. Do you think this might eliminate some arguments?

Get Godly Counsel

> Plans fail for lack of counsel, but with many
> advisers they succeed. (Prov. 15:22 NIV)

> The way of a fool is right in his own eyes, but
> a wise man is he who listens to counsel. (Prov.
> 12:15 NASB)

God often reveals wisdom to us through the advice of
believers. We desperately need people in our lives who can give
us wise counsel. If you decide to seek the advice of a financial
adviser, choose someone who knows what Scripture says about
money and understands how to apply it to your life.

But don't end there when making major financial decisions.
Find one or two spiritually mature people, and ask them these
three questions.

> Are any of the options I am considering outside the
> boundaries of God's Word?
>
> What do you think is the wise thing for me to do?
>
> What decision would you make if you were me?

Have a Long-Term Perspective

> Do not lay up for yourselves treasures on earth,
> where moth and rust destroy and where thieves
> break in and steal, but lay up for yourselves
> treasures in heaven, where neither moth nor rust
> destroys and where thieves do not break in or steal.
> For where your treasure is, there will your heart be
> also. (Matt. 6:19–21 ESV)

When we see life on earth as preparation for our ultimate
destination of heaven, we choose material possessions carefully.

And we avoid allowing the temporal to distract us from the eternal. C. S. Lewis says, "Our father refreshes us on the journey with some pleasant inns, but will not encourage us to mistake them for home."[23]

A Kansas State University study on the benefits of a long-term perspective, states, "If you are more willing to pick later, larger rewards rather than taking the immediate payoff, you are more future-minded than present-minded."[24] This is exactly what God calls us to do—pick the later and larger rewards of heaven over the immediate payoff of this world.

After almost two decades as a financial planner, I can say with certainty there is a direct correlation between the length of one's perspective and the quality of his or her financial decisions. The longer a person's outlook, the better the choices he or she will make. The ideal long-term viewpoint is eternal. But even a five- or ten-year outlook will result in better outcomes than a view focused on today.

Be Willing to Wait

> A faithful man will abound with blessings, but he
> who makes haste to be rich will not go unpunished.
> A man with an evil eye hastens after wealth, and
> does not know that want will come upon him.
> (Prov. 28:20, 22 NASB)

Consider waiting at least twenty-four hours before making any major purchase, since impatience often leads to poor financial decisions. One of our society's most successful marketing techniques is to use the pressure of time. "Act now!" "Only for the first 100 callers!" "You must buy today!" "This is a once in a lifetime opportunity!" These are all temptations to buy on emotion rather than wisdom. It is better to pay more and have peace of mind than to get a deal on impulse and be filled with regret.

Be Careful Not to Presume on the Future

> Come now, you who say, "Today or tomorrow, we
> will go to such and such a city, and spend a year
> there and engage in business and make a profit."
> Yet you do not know what your life will be like
> tomorrow. You are just a vapor that appears for a
> little while and then vanishes away. Instead, you
> ought to say, "If the Lord wills, we will live and
> also do this or that." (Jas. 4:13–15 NASB)

It is dangerous to make purchases contingent on unrealistic,
unknown, or unlikely future events. The classic example of a
presumptuous purchase is buying a house under the assumptions
future income will be much higher, that two incomes will last
forever, or that property values will always go up. As the last
decade in real estate has taught us, it is precarious to assume what
tomorrow will bring.

Watch Out for Anxiety

> For this reason I say to you, do not be worried
> about your life, as to what you will eat or what you
> will drink; nor for your body, as to what you shall
> put on. Is not life more than food, and the body
> than clothing? (Matt. 6:25 NASB)

> Be anxious for nothing, but in everything by
> prayer and supplication with thanksgiving let your
> requests be made known to God. And the peace
> of God, which surpasses all comprehension, will
> guard your hearts and your minds in Christ Jesus.
> (Phil. 4:6–7 NASB)

God tells us to be anxious for nothing. We obey this command by avoiding financial decisions that create worry. Even a financial decision that produces more money may not be worth the anxiety that is caused along the way. Financial peace will not come solely from more money. In fact, it is often the opposite that occurs. Listen to what some of the richest men in our country's history have said.

> I have made many millions, but they have brought me no happiness. (John D. Rockefeller)
>
> The care of $200,000,000 is enough to kill anyone. There is no pleasure in it. (W. H. Vanderbilt)
>
> I am the most miserable man on earth. (John Jacob Astor)
>
> I was happier when doing a mechanics job. (Henry Ford)
>
> Millionaires seldom smile. (Andrew Carnegie)

Make Decisions Consistent with Your Goals

> Commit your works to the Lord, and your plans will be established. The mind of man plans his way, but the Lord directs his steps. (Prov. 16:3, 9 NASB)
>
> The steps of a man are established by the Lord; and He delights in his way. (Ps. 37:23 NASB)

Goals serve as our road map as we make financial decisions. Ask, "How does this decision fit with what I say is most important?"

A few years ago, a client called to ask my opinion about buying a new car, which he could get for a really good deal (by the way, no one ever calls and says, "I have this opportunity to get totally ripped off!"). There was certainly nothing wrong with him buying a new car. But in a meeting a few months earlier, he and his wife had written out their five most important financial objectives for the year, and a new car was not one of them.

I reminded him of what they had decided and asked if buying a new car was now a higher priority. He thought for a moment and replied, "No, our other goals are still more important." My role in that situation was to keep them accountable, reminding him what he and his wife had predetermined was most important. They made a better decision because their goals were written down.

As I would soon find out, even with well-defined goals, the challenges of life can make it difficult to stay focused on what matters most.

Chapter 4

The Power to Make Wealth

T he phone call came at 11:06 a.m. on May 2, 2011. I knew as soon as I heard the voice on the other end. It was my doctor. The doctor never makes these calls unless the news is bad. A nurse calls with the good news. He said, "Mr. Gum, you have prostate cancer."

They are always so matter of fact, which I suppose is necessary when you have to deliver such horrific news. At forty-four years old, I had the cancer I thought only grandfathers were supposed to get. I didn't want to tell Susan over the phone, so I headed home. She was not there. So for the next forty-five minutes, I sat in my upstairs office, waiting for her, contemplating how I was going to communicate this life-altering information. I didn't know it at the time, but saying those words to her would be the hardest part of the entire cancer ordeal for me.

About a month earlier, I had been in for an overdue physical at the urging of my wife, who was worried about my cholesterol. Fortunately, my cholesterol was fine, but the doctor saw an abnormality in my PSA test. (Most doctors don't test the PSA until age fifty, but mine began testing at age forty, which explains that one charge my insurance company would never cover from my annual physical!) Because I had no family history, he felt certain it was nothing serious. But as a precaution, he sent me to an urologist. The phone call was from the urologist, with the result of the biopsy (not a fun process!) that had been performed the previous week.

Over the next month, I learned more about the prostate and cancer than I ever cared to know. During a visit to the Johns Hopkins Medical Center in Baltimore, a very experienced surgeon looked at me and said, "This isn't your dad's prostate cancer. Yours is a fast growing cancer, and if it spreads outside of your prostate, there is not much we can do. We need to act quickly and aggressively." And they did. My prostate was removed in what turned out to be a fairly complicated surgery on June 20.

Later that week, we made the flight back to Charlotte, and I began the long road to recovery at home. The instructions were simple—stay in bed for a month but walk as much as I could. I never was quite able to reconcile those two orders.

One of my first mornings at home, eighteen-year-old Griffin stuck his head inside my bedroom. With much envy, he asked, "Dad, isn't it great that all you have to do today is watch movies?"

I replied, "Yes, yes I guess that is great." And it was good for the first few days. I watched several movies I had wanted to see. I used the cell phone from my bed to call my wife in the other room when I needed something. I spent a lot of time caring for myself and concentrating on my recovery. In short, it was as if I had been given permission to be completely self-absorbed. My world consisted of me.

I had lofty plans for what I was going to accomplish during my recovery. I was excited to read those four books that had been on my bookshelf for too long. I was hoping to complete a big marketing project for work that never seemed to fit into my schedule. And I was excited to prepare lots of Bible studies for the boy's high school discipleship group I led. But the combination of the pain from surgery and my foggy brain from the lingering anesthesia made it a struggle to concentrate for more than a couple of minutes. I would read a page only to realize I had no idea what I just read. I got almost nothing done. My routine quickly became utterly meaningless and void of any hint of joy.

I was going crazy. I was in a dark place. As I cried over my frustration one morning, God impressed on my heart one of the clearest lessons He has ever taught me. It was as if He said, "This is what it is like when you are focused on yourself and are unproductive." I don't think I will ever forget that moment. I had a great excuse to be lazy. After all, I was essentially confined to my bed. My days consisted of post-op care and aspirations of walking to the mailbox and back. But the lesson was so very powerful. As I slowly regained my health and energy over the following months, I was reminded over and over again how wonderful it is to turn our focus away from ourselves and to be productive for the Lord. I came to realize this is one of the greatest blessings of work.

Do you dream of when you no longer have to work? Do you live for your days off? If so, then like me, you need to view work differently.

The world says the purpose of work is to earn money so that we can buy things. Apparently, we learn this at a young age, as I found out a few years back, when Griffin was six and compiling his Christmas list. He came outside, where I was doing yard work, held up *my* credit card, and said, "I want one of these for Christmas."

I said, "You can't have a credit card."

"Why not?" he asked.

"Because you don't have a job," I stated. He went back inside, where he continued the conversation with Susan.

"What's a job?"

"Why do you ask?" she responded.

"Because Dad said I have to have a job to get one of these for Christmas," Griffin explained, holding up the credit card.

Griffin thought that if you worked, you got money to buy things, and that looked pretty good to him.

Susan said, "Well, he's right. You do have to have a job to have a credit card."

Now Griffin was a pretty quick thinker, so he shot back, "Do you have a job?"

Griffin did not understand the proper definition of work. As we will see later, Susan did indeed have a very important job!

Culture tells us work is a means to an end, a way to achieve self-sufficiency and financial independence. We work because we need money. As a result, most of us see our jobs as a necessary evil. After all, we throw parties for people who stop working.

I often ask my clients, "If you no longer had a need for income, what would you do?" Contemplating this is fascinating, because it separates work from money. It reveals our passions, what we really care about and enjoy.

I receive a variety of answers, but most give responses that are different from their current jobs. When I ask why they are not pursuing the vocation of their passion, their typical answer is, "What I would really enjoy doing does not pay enough." We typically choose our occupation based on the income it produces, a way to support our current and future lifestyles. I want to challenge this widespread view of work.

The Biblical Reasons for Work

We Have an Innate, God-Given Drive to Be Productive

In order to understand this, we have to start with the beginning, with the first work that was ever done, all the way back to Genesis.

> Now no shrub of the field was yet in the earth, and
> no plant of the field had yet sprouted, for the LORD

God had not sent rain upon the earth; and there was
no man to cultivate the ground. Then the LORD
God took the man and put him into the garden of
Eden to cultivate it and keep it. (Gen. 2:5, 15 NASB)

The timing of this verse is intriguing, because God gave
Adam this "work ordinance" of caring for the garden before sin
entered the world. This means work is good and part of what
God designed us to do in His perfect creation. Work is not a
punishment for sin; it just became hard as a result of sin (Gen.
3:17–19). At some point, we may accumulate more money than we
need. But because the ultimate goal of our toil is being productive
for the Lord, we should remain involved in some form of labor or
service as long as we are able.

Work Provides Fulfillment

Whatever you do, do your work heartily, as for the
Lord rather than for men; knowing that from the Lord
you will receive the reward of the inheritance. It is
the Lord Christ whom you serve. (Col. 3:23, 24 NASB)

We experience true fulfillment when we use our God-given
gifts and skills to serve God. Our satisfaction is never complete
when we toil for men and women, or when our primary motivation
is financial security. This is why retirement to a life of leisure is so
dangerous; it lacks the fulfillment working provides.

Work Presents an Opportunity to Provide
for Our Families and Others

But if anyone does not provide for his own, and
especially for those of his household, he has denied
the faith and is worse than an unbeliever. (1 Tim.
5:8 NASB)

> At the present time your plenty will supply what
> they need, so that in turn their plenty will supply
> what you need. (2 Cor. 8:14 NIV)

Providing for our family and sharing our surplus with others are the objectives. Too often, our view of work is selfish; it is about our own goals and desires. How can I make enough to buy that new car or a second home? When can I retire? Instead, like Christ commands, be mindful of others by caring and providing for them. One of the greatest ways we show our love for God is through our obedience.

Work Provides an Environment to Live Out Our Christian Life

Even if our job is rather mundane, there is always eternal significance in the relationships we have with people as a result of our work.

> You are the light of the world. A city set on a hill
> cannot be hidden; nor does anyone light a lamp
> and put it under a basket, but on the lampstand,
> and it gives light to all who are in the house. Let
> your light shine before men in such a way that
> they may see your good works, and glorify to your
> Father who is in heaven. (Matt. 5:14–16 NASB)

All work gives us the opportunity to let our lights shine through our good works and love for others, bringing glory to our Father.

Scripture Commands Us to Work

> For even when we were with you, we used to give
> you this order: if anyone is not willing to work,
> then he is not to eat, either. (2 Thess. 3:10 NASB)

This is simple. If we are able to work, we need to work.

A New Definition of Work and Income

After studying what Scripture says, we can define work differently: *Work is the physical and mental energy exerted to be productive in what God has called and equipped us to do.* This new definition of work applies to everyone: the student, the hourly worker, the business owner, the executive, the missionary, the stay-at-home mom, and the retiree.

A Change in Focus

In the late 1800s, a man was reading the morning newspaper. To his horror, he read his own name in the obituary section. His brother had recently died, and the newspaper printed his obituary by mistake. The headline read, "Dynamite King Dies." It went on to call him the "merchant of death," since he was the chemist who invented dynamite.

His innovation was one of the first weapons of mass destruction and was used by governments to kill people in unprecedented numbers. Even though he was extremely wealthy as a result of his work, he was deeply shaken by this assessment of his life. Given a second chance to do good, he committed to using his fortune and the remainder of his days to reward people whose work and accomplishments benefited humankind.

His name was Alfred Nobel, and the award program he developed is the Nobel Peace Prize. Nobel lived the contrasting definitions of work. The first was self-focused; the second was about others.[25]

Do you see the difference? The world views work as a means to an end (financial freedom) and yearns for the day when it is no longer required. In contrast, Scripture teaches that great fulfillment comes from labor, because it is part of what we are created to do. It is not something we should try to quit as soon as we can. Service for the Lord is something we should always do in some form.

The biblical view of work may or may not involve income, since money is not the only purpose of work. Instead, the primary focus is to be productive for the Lord. God did not pay Adam for his initial work, but I am certain he garnered great satisfaction from caring for the garden and pleasing his Master. Never in Scripture is the aim of work portrayed as self-serving. It is always focused on others—working as unto the Lord, providing for our family, and providing for others.

Many of my clients have reached the point where they are no longer in need of earned income. This is a great opportunity for them to pray, "Lord, in light of the fact that I no longer need earned income, how can I be most productive for You?" The nature of work may change, but the need to be productive remains. This is why the lesson I learned during my prostate cancer recovery was so powerful. It made me yearn to get back to work so that I could be productive and get the focus off myself. A proper view of work does that!

God Owns It All

"The silver is Mine, and the gold is Mine," declares the LORD of hosts. (Hag. 2:8 NASB)

The earth is the LORD'S, and all it contains, the world, and those who dwell in it. (Ps. 24:1 NASB)

This principle is critical to understanding work and income. If we miss this, we miss it all.

One of the greatest missing teachings in the American church today is the reminder to men and women that nothing we have belongs to us. (Gordon McDonald)

Only when we understand that God owns everything are we able to surrender our misconceptions of ownership. Even for mature believers, one of the last areas of surrender to the Lord is money. If we fail to recognize God's ownership by holding money and possessions tightly, we expose ourselves to the very serious dangers of loving money.

Ownership matters. When we own something, we can do with it as we please. If we are caring for another's property, we do not have that same privilege. We become stewards, required to faithfully care for the borrowed items in the owner's best interest.

How do we become faithful? We recognize everything we have is God's. Then we act on this truth by handling our wealth for His benefit. Understanding and obeying what we find in Scripture is the guide, since God reveals how His money should be managed in the Bible!

God Gives the Power

Recognizing God's ownership leads us to one additional certainty; He is responsible for the wealth we have. This is not a popular view, but it is true. We think we are in control and that it is our education, skill, and hard work that create wealth and give us the ability to be rich. But this is not what the Bible says.

> It is the blessing of the LORD that makes rich, and He adds no sorrow to it. (Prov. 10:22 NASB)

> But you shall remember the LORD your God, for it is He who is giving you power to make wealth, that He may confirm His covenant which He swore to your fathers, as it is this day. (Deut. 8:18 NASB)

God grants the power to make wealth and has the ultimate authority over how much we earn. Since God owns it all, He can both give and take what He wants when He wants. We experience great freedom when we understand our responsibility is to work hard for the Lord, depend on Him for our needs, and live within the income and wealth He allows.

The Balance of Work

In his book *Your Money Counts*, Howard Dayton writes, "People usually lean to one of two extremes: they either work as little as possible because work is unpleasant, or they tend to work all the time because it becomes overwhelmingly important. Scripture affirms the value of hard work but teaches that we should have a balance in work."[26]

Falling into one of these excesses—working too little or working too much—is usually caused by having an improper view of work. Charles Spurgeon said, "All men must work, but no man should work beyond his physical and intellectual ability nor beyond the hours which nature allots. No net result of good to the individual or to the race comes of any artificial prolonging of the day at either end. Work while it is day. When night comes, rest."[27]

To determine our allotted time, we must establish priorities and set boundaries. And we must have faith. Like many of you, I have had occasions during my career when there was more work to do than there was time. In my first few years at RB&Co., I was supporting another manager as his financial planner while also trying to build my own client base.

The days were never long enough. I went to work early, came home for a quick dinner, and went back to the office until late at night. Some nights I did not get home until after Susan put our young boys to bed. I still remember her saying, "If you are going to get home right after I put everybody to bed, you might as well just stay at work!" She was right.

When I was at work, I felt like I should be home. And when I was at home, I felt I should be at work. I was hopelessly conflicted. During this time, I was in a small-group Bible study with one of the pastors at my church. He sensed my frustration over the lack of balance in my life and invited me to lunch. During our meal, he asked me about my priorities and what was most important in my life. I gave him the standard answer of, "God, family, and work."

He replied, "The way you spend your time does not seem to match those priorities." It was hard to hear, but I knew he was right. I just did not know what to do about it. Then he asked me how much I could work without compromising my family's position as a higher priority than my job.

I determined I could go into work early and still work some long hours, but it was really important to eat dinner with my family, help put the kids to bed, and not go back to the office at night. I needed to be engaged with my wife and kids during the evening.

But I still would not have enough time to complete all my work, especially the marketing aspect of my job. Then came his challenge. "Determine the amount of time you can spend at work to maintain your priorities, and trust God with the rest."

He went on to say, "God can bring you new clients." It was a great lesson. Since work is about so much more than what I can produce, it gave me a great freedom to know I needed to work hard, but God was ultimately in control of the results. God honored that decision to add balance to my life.

If you have a variable time job, set reasonable time parameters that protect your higher priorities. Do your best during those hours, and trust God for the rest.

One additional tip for maintaining balance in your life is to make sure you take a day off each week. Scripture is emphatic about accomplishing our work in six days (Ex. 34:21). We are created to need a day off. I find I accomplish more during a week with a day of true rest than I do working seven days without a break. God knows how we function best.

Keep It in Perspective

A couple I know illustrates much of what this chapter is about. He works in a counseling ministry, and she is a schoolteacher. They are wonderful Christian parents, raising three of the finest kids I know. In short, they have a great marriage and family. But money is a constant struggle for them.

In their careers, they will probably never make enough to keep up with their fast-spending, suburban neighbors. When I recently told them I have several clients with enormous net worths who would immediately trade places with them, they were stunned.

"Why would these wealthy individuals trade places with us?" they asked.

"Because you have what money can't buy: a deep relationship with Christ, a great marriage, sweet relationships with your children—who are believers—and true fulfillment and purpose in your work."

Having a biblical view of work keeps our focus on what is most important. Work brings significance when we are productive in what God has called and equipped us to do, regardless of whether it results in tremendous income or not. If we see work as an opportunity to live and share the Christian life, we will focus more on others, realize income is not the primary goal, and be much more likely to have a balanced lifestyle. Join me in this pursuit to see work differently!

CHAPTER 5

GIVING—DON'T MISS THE BLESSING

When it comes to money and the Bible, the area of giving creates the most debate and disagreement. Conduct an Internet search for "Should Christians tithe?" and you will discover hundreds of articles, many with sharply conflicting opinions. What a disappointment that so much of what is written about being charitable appears argumentative or legalistic. As believers, we should experience joy and freedom in our giving, not the binding nature of compulsion.

After years of studying what the Bible teaches about giving, I have reached a simple, nondebatable conclusion: God calls His children to be generous!

> Instruct those who are rich in this present world not to be conceited or to fix their hope on the uncertainty of riches, but on God, who richly supplies us with all things to enjoy. Instruct them to do good, to be rich in good works, *to be generous*

and ready to share, storing up for themselves the treasure of a good foundation for the future, so that they may take hold of that which is life indeed. (1 Tim. 6:17–19 NASB, emphasis added)

Now he who supplies seed to the sower and bread for food will also supply and increase your store of seed and will enlarge the harvest of your righteousness. You will be enriched in every way *so that you can be generous on every occasion,* and through us your generosity will result in thanksgiving to God. (2 Cor. 9:10–11 NIV, emphasis added)

If anyone has material possessions and sees a brother or sister in need but has no pity on them, how can the love of God be in that person? Dear children, let us not love with words or speech *but with actions and in truth.* (1 John 3:17–18 NIV, emphasis added)

When the Bible references financial stewardship, faithfulness is always framed in generosity. It seems logical to assume Christians would give abundantly. Unfortunately, when we are viewed as a group, this is not true.

Sobering Statistics

- Only 9.4 percent of all Christians donate 10 percent or more each year.[26]

- The average American Christian gives 2.9 percent of their income to charity.[28]

- The average amount of giving by church members to their churches in 2010 was 2.4 percent. This was the lowest level during the time period of 1968–2010. To put it in perspective, since 1968, personal income has risen 130 percent in inflation-adjusted dollars.[29]

- "Born-again" Christians donated an average of $1,971 to all nonprofits and churches in 2007.[30]

- Forty-five percent of "committed" Christians give away less than 2 percent of their income each year.[26]

- Twenty percent of all US Christians give nothing to church, parachurch, or nonreligious charities.[26]

- Higher income–earning Christians do not give more (as a percentage of their income) than lower income–earning Christians.[26]

- A review of eleven denominations from 1921 to 2010 determined that members gave a higher percentage of their income to the church in 1933 (the Great Depression) than they did in 2010.[27]

Looking at these statistics, we can safely say we are not meeting the standard of generosity God calls us to. I recently heard a pastor say, "The good news is that we have all of the money we need to fund the church, fulfill the Great Commission, and end poverty. The bad news is that most of it is still in your pockets!"

So what does it mean to be generous? Is it simply to tithe? Don McClaren writes, "The tithe can become an idol to set upon a pedestal to admire. It is often a dangerously tempting resting place rather than a minimal starting place. Much of the Christian community thinks of tithing as a high and lofty perch that only a few radicals have reached after years of struggle, rather than seeing it as the bottom or beginning place."[31]

Let's propose a new standard of giving; 10 percent is a great place to start and a bad place to end. Why? Because some of us need to give more than 10 percent in order to be generous! Scripture tells us to give in proportion to how we much we have, and that we have been blessed with more so we can give more (2 Cor. 8:11). In 2 Corinthians 8:3, some even gave, "beyond their ability." What seems generous for one is not necessarily generous for all.

C. S. Lewis made a profound conclusion when he said, "I do not believe we can settle how much we ought to give. I am afraid the only safe role is to give more than we can spare."[32]

Why Give Generously?

Giving Is an Act of Worship

> *Honor* the LORD from your wealth, and from the first of all your produce; (Prov. 3:9 NASB, emphasis added)

> I have received full payment and have more than enough. I am amply supplied, now that I have received from Epaphroditus the gifts you sent. They are *a fragrant offering, an acceptable sacrifice, pleasing to God.* (Phil. 4:18 NIV, emphasis added)

Throughout the Old Testament, bringing tithes and offerings were an important form of worship. Even in the New Testament, Paul called the believers' gifts, "a fragrant offering, an acceptable sacrifice, pleasing to God."

We worship when we give, recognizing God owns it all and thanking Him for His provision. He is the Creator of heaven and earth and the author of everything that is good. He even sent His only Son, Jesus, to die on the cross for our sins so that we might have eternal life! Our regular giving is a tangible reminder of God's authority and our need to praise and worship Him.

Giving Meets Needs Close to God's Heart

When the boys were younger, we began to teach them about money and giving. I remember one occasion when I gave seven-year-old Xander his $2 allowance and asked, "How much do you think you should give to God?"

Looking a bit perplexed, he reluctantly answered, "All of it?"

He was relieved when I said, "Why don't you start with twenty cents?"

With big eyes, he asked, "How do I get the money to God?"

With Xander's question in mind, let's look at how we actually can give to God by giving to those close to His heart.

God has established two specific groups who are tremendously important to Him—those in ministry and those who are poor and neglected.

Those in Ministry

In the same way, the Lord has commanded that those who preach the gospel should receive their living from the gospel. (1 Cor. 9:14 NIV)

> Nevertheless, the one who receives instruction in the word should share all good things with their instructor. (Gal. 6:6 NIV)

> The elders who direct the affairs of the church well are worthy of double honor, especially those whose work is preaching and teaching. For Scripture says, "Do not muzzle an ox while it is treading out the grain," and "The worker deserves his wages." (1 Tim. 5:17–18 NIV)

Without a doubt, we must support those in ministry, which includes churches and charities doing God's work. There are thousands of these from which to choose. Here are a few tips to help you decide which ones should receive your donations:

- Give where you and your family are receiving teaching and blessing, which should always include your local church.
- Give to help fulfill the Great Commission.
- Give where you have a passion.
- Give locally, nationally, and internationally.
- Give to ministries who do their work in the name of Christ and practice good stewardship.

Some churches teach that our tithe (10 percent) should go to the church, and that we should support other ministries and missionaries with offerings above our tithe. This admirable practice comes from Old Testament teachings. The New Testament encourages us to "give as we have purposed in our heart, not grudgingly or *under compulsion*, for God loves a cheerful giver" (2 Corinthians 9:2, emphasis added). It seems legalistic, then, to say that 10 percent *must* go to our local church. As believers, we *do* have a strong obligation to sustain the church, which is the bride of Christ. And with the average Christian only giving 2.4 percent of his or her income to the church, our room for improvement is substantial.

Here is the challenge. Let's make it a priority to be purposeful and plentiful in our support of all those doing the Lord's work in ministry.

The Poor and Neglected

> But whoever has the world's goods, and sees his brother in need and closes his heart against him, how does the love of God abide in him? (1 John 3:17 NASB)

He who gives to the poor will never want, but he who shuts his eyes will have many curses. (Prov. 28:27 NASB)

You shall generously give to him, and your heart shall not be grieved when you give to him, because for this thing the LORD your God will bless you in all your work and in all your undertakings. "For the poor will never cease to be in the land; therefore I command you, saying, `You shall freely open your hand to your brother, to your needy and poor in your land.'" (Deut. 15:10–11 NASB)

Share with the Lord's people who are in need. Practice hospitality. (Rom. 12:13 NIV)

John answered, "Anyone who has two shirts should share with the one who has none, and anyone who has food should do the same." (Luke 3:11 NIV)

God's passion about giving to the poor is strong and consistent in His Word. Yet our giving to those with the greatest needs is typically one the most ignored areas of our benevolence. We often think wrongly that caring for the poor is the responsibility of the government, but the need for state and federal programs would be greatly reduced or even eliminated if Christians gave to the poor as Scripture teaches.

The scope of the needs of the poor around the world is overwhelming. We know we cannot help everyone, but as Pastor Andy Stanley says, "Do for one what you wish you could do for everyone."[33]

My family's *one* is Evelyn Castillo. I met Evelyn on a visit to an orphanage in the Dominican Republic in January of 2008. Griffin and I played games with a group of kids for several hours that day, but it was ten-year-old Evelyn who captured our hearts. Later that week, we learned most of the kids in the orphanage were in desperate need of monthly sponsors to cover their basic necessities.

We immediately began to sponsor Evelyn. We started writing letters back and forth and sending her gifts for her birthday and Christmas. Everyone in our family has met Evelyn, who is especially drawn to Susan.

When we arrive at the orphanage for our yearly visit, she runs and jumps into our arms, crying, "Mi Americanos, Mi Americanos!" Even though our monthly donations aren't much, they have been substantial, even life-changing for her. We discovered she has a serious illness, with symptoms that can be treated by vitamins almost impossible for the orphanage to obtain. But they are very easy for us to purchase.

We have given her a Bible and been able to encourage her faith in Jesus. Over the years, the bond between us has become quite strong. We love her, and she loves our family and is deeply appreciative of our involvement in her life.

On our most recent visit, Xander and I had fun helping Evelyn with her broken English as she helped us with our pitiful Spanish. I was trying to say her full name, Evelyn Castillo, over and over with the correct Latino enunciation with only moderate success when she interrupted me. In her sweet accent, she said, "My name is Evelyn Castillo Gum!" I gave her a hug and told her we loved her (one of the few phrases I can say well in Spanish). She feels a part of our family, which is a wonderful gift for a young girl who doesn't have one of her own. We experience pure joy as we help provide for her. Do for one what you wish you could do for everyone!

Remember Xander's question? We are "rich toward God," showing our love for Him, when we are generous with those in ministry and those who are neglected. Think about it. One of the best ways someone can love us is to invest in our kids, especially when they are in need. It is the same way with God. What a great privilege to be used as part of God's provision for those close to His heart.

We Receive Blessings

Some find it uncomfortable and self-serving to consider individual reward or benefit as any part of our motivation for giving. But God consistently promises that He will abundantly bless those who are generous. If He did not want this to be part of our incentive, He would have just told us to give without ever mentioning the rewards. Instead, He talks about our receiving blessings both in this world and the one to come. Embracing this truth from God's Word is critical to changing how we view giving.

Blessings in This Life

> Honor the LORD with your wealth, with the firstfruits of all your crops; then *your barns will be filled to overflowing, and your vats will brim over with new wine.* (Prov. 3:9, 10 NASB, emphasis added)

> Give generously to them and so without a grudging heart; then because of this the Lord your God will *bless you in all your work and in everything you put your hand to.* (Deut. 15:10 NASB, emphasis added)

> He who gives to the poor *will never want,* but he who shuts his eyes will have many curses. (Prov. 28:27 NASB, emphasis added)

> There is one who scatters, yet *increases all the more,* and there is one who withholds what is justly due, but it results only in want. The generous man will be *prosperous,* and he who waters *will himself be watered.* (Prov. 11:24, 25 NASB, emphasis added)

> Give, and it will be given to you. *A good measure, pressed down, shaken together and running over, will*

be poured into your lap. For with the measure you use, it will be measured to you. (Luke 6:38 NIV, emphasis added)

In everything I did, I showed you that by this kind of hard work we must help the weak, remembering the words the Lord Jesus himself said: "It is *more blessed to give than to receive.*" (Acts 20:35 NIV, emphasis added)

These verses show the consequences we suffer for being stingy:

- We will have many curses.
- We will never be content.

And the blessings we enjoy from being generous:

- We have everything we need.
- We will be filled with joy, and God will bless our work.
- We will be content.
- We will be refreshed.
- We will receive kindness and help from others.
- We will experience joy from our giving.

These verses do not promote the "prosperity gospel." The blessings God promises are much more valuable and varied than simply material wealth. One of the creative blessings God bestows when we are generous is peace of mind. At first glance, it does not make sense that giving what we have to others would result in our greater comfort. But it does!

Scripture alone should be enough to convince us, but this truth was reinforced in a powerful way when I recently decided to place my clients into two groups: the group who suffered financial anxiety and the group who possessed financial peace of mind. I was curious to discover what the clients in the peace of mind group had in common.

To my initial surprise, almost everyone in this group possessed one very distinct characteristic. What do you think it was? They were the most generous and cheerful givers. It had nothing to do with their salary, net worth, or size of their retirement accounts. Peace of mind is a blessing of generosity!

Blessings in the Life to Come

> Sell your possessions and give to the poor. Provide purses for yourselves that will not wear out, *a treasure in heaven that will never fail,* where no thief comes near and no moth destroys. (Luke 12:33 NIV, emphasis added)

> Command them to do good, to be rich in good deeds, and to be generous and willing to share. In this way they *will lay up treasure for themselves as a firm foundation for the coming age, so that they may take hold of the life that is truly life.* (1 Tim. 6:18–19 NIV, emphasis added)

We must understand that there is more to this life than this life. The way we live now impacts how we will live in heaven. We can exchange the wealth of this temporal world for benefits in heaven that will last forever. You can read more about this amazing truth in Randy Alcorn's book, *The Treasure Principle: Discovering the Secret of Joyful Giving.*

God promises benefits to the generous both in this world (contentment, joy, kindness from others) and in the world to come (treasure in heaven). When we fully comprehend these truths about giving, we should be inspired to be exceedingly generous!

Why Don't We Give More?

Looking at the statistics, we are not being generous. Because Ronald Blue & Co. helps Christians become financially free to assist in fulfilling the Great Commission, we often ask, "Why don't Christians give more?"

There are many reasons—financial problems, lack of trust, absence of vision, and selfishness. Most Christians want to give more than they do. The problem is not one of desire but of priorities, as a multitude of goals compete for our dollars. Daily life is expensive; taxes are high, college is costly, and the amount needed for retirement is daunting. While most believe giving is an important objective, statistics indicate churches and charities only receive our leftovers. Why does this happen?

We Don't Read

Statistics reveal that the most generous Christians are those who are serious about their faith. Research from *View from the Pew* shows that those who read their Bibles at least four days each week are twice as likely to give 10 percent or more of their income to God.[34] Increased Bible reading and significant giving are highly correlated, because what God says about benevolence is clear, consistent, and compelling. In order to contribute more of our dollars, we need to read and believe God's Word.

We Don't Plan

Research suggests lack of planning is the primary reason Christians don't give more.

> Each of you should give what you have *decided* in your heart to give, not reluctantly or under compulsion, for God loves a cheerful giver. (2 Cor. 9:7 NIV, emphasis added)

On the *first* day of every week each one of you is
to put aside and save, as he may prosper, so that
no collections be made when I come. (1 Cor. 16:2
NASB, emphasis added)

Honor the LORD from your wealth, And from the
first of all your produce; (Prov. 3:9 NASB, emphasis
added)

Paul's use of the word "decided" carries with it an element of
planning. Scripture explains that certain spending priorities are
more important than others. This is why the chapters in this book
are sequenced as they are. Since giving is our first priority in the
priority order of spending, it is important to determine our giving
before we make other spending decisions. If we have not purposed
our giving in advance, we end up contributing our leftovers.

Financial planners routinely recommend families
automatically deduct their retirement and savings amounts from
their paychecks to ensure their savings goals are accomplished.
Consider implementing this same strategy for your regular
charitable giving by utilizing bank bill pay or automatic payment
plans. At first, this might seem a bit uncomfortable, but planning
in this way guarantees we will achieve our giving goals by
making them a first priority.

Our regular giving is a tangible reminder of God's authority
and our need to praise and worship Him. The manner in which we
give should not influence our worship. If we struggle to worship
without actually placing something in the offering plate, put in
few dollars, a small check, or a donation card that some churches
provide for their automatic givers.

The Bible directs us to give first, regularly, and cheerfully.
These are all more likely to occur when we intentionally plan
our giving.

Lifestyle Generosity

First Timothy 6:18 proclaims, "Instruct them to do good, to be rich in good works, to be generous and ready to share." Second Corinthians 9:11 explains, "so that you can be generous on every occasion." Generosity is more than just the money we give on Sundays; it should permeate our daily lives, defining who we are. As followers of Christ, we should display lifestyle generosity. Lifestyle generosity is showing our love for God and others with our money and our actions.

> Dear children, let us not love with words or speech
> but with actions and in truth. (1 John 3:18 NIV)

My friend Ruth is a perfect example of practicing lifestyle generosity. She and her husband, Allen, spent over fifty years in ministry. During all of those years, they were faithful, cheerful, and intentional givers with both their money and their actions.

In addition to their church giving, they shared a passion to use money to spread the Gospel to some of the darkest corners of the world. Albania was one such country. For fifteen years, they prayed for this country to become open to the Gospel. When missionaries were finally allowed into Albania, Allen and Ruth visited to find additional ways to invest their dollars to reach the lost.

After living in California for forty years, they retired to Charlotte in 1999 to be close to their son-in-law and daughter, who had recently given birth to a baby with special needs. It was during this time that I had the privilege to know them and to see their giving spirits.

Now a widow, Ruth remains incredibly involved in God's work, and her life is still marked by extraordinary generosity. She continues to give a significant amount of money to her church and ministries around the world. She routinely gives away 15 percent of her income to charity; in one recent year she gave away almost 50 percent! At eighty-two years young, she still supports and stays involved in the work of organizations doing amazing deeds in the name of Christ around the globe. What really amazes me is how generous Ruth is with her entire life, not just her money.

Recently, she inspired me with the story of a young Muslim couple, Ahmed and Meriem. Last December, Ruth drove to the local mall to buy a Christmas gift for her granddaughter. As she entered the boutique, she noticed the clerk, Meriem, was crying. Ruth immediately went over to comfort her. While Meriem had been helping another customer a few minutes earlier, her wallet was stolen from behind the counter. Although she had lost her credit cards, driver's license, and checks, what really upset her was the loss of the irreplaceable pictures of her family from Morocco. Ruth empathized with her loss and hugged her. Meriem was truly touched by Ruth's kindness. If it ended here, it would be a nice story, because Ruth already did what most would not.

But it did not end here. The next week, Ruth made a special trip back to the store to check on her new friend and see if her wallet had been returned. Meriem was amazed Ruth remembered and cared so much. Even though the wallet had not been recovered, Ruth's visit encouraged Meriem.

Ruth continued to go back to the store every week, which always delighted Meriem. On one of the visits, Meriem shared how she and Ahmed were new to town and quite lonely. And they encountered people who were hostile toward their appearance and heritage. Some would even come into the store to shout, "Go back to your own country!" Ruth was one of the only people who cared about them.

After four months of these visits, Meriem had exciting news to share with Ruth. She was pregnant with her first child! Ruth was ecstatic for Meriem and had an idea.

She asked, "Do you know what a baby shower is?"

After explaining this American tradition, Ruth asked, "May I have a baby shower for you?"

Meriem agreed to Ruth's offer, although she had only one friend to invite. Ruth contacted some of her friends from church and was thrilled when they enthusiastically agreed to participate in this celebration for a complete stranger. A few weeks later, Ruth and her friends had a fabulous time at Meriem's party. Meriem was overwhelmed by the generous gifts given to her by people she did not even know.

Meriem was so appreciative of Ruth's friendship that she invited Ruth to her apartment for tea. Knowing how significant an invitation to one's home was in Meriem's culture, Ruth was honored to accept. During their visit, Meriem shared from her heart, "Ruth, you are our family."

Ruth continued to see Meriem at the store and at her apartment. When Meriem delivered her baby girl, Ruth was the first one they called, inviting her to come to the hospital to see their newborn daughter.

When Ruth arrived, the nurse asked, "Are you family?"

Ruth paused and then answered, "Yes, yes I think am."

Without hesitation, the nurse escorted Ruth down the hall to see Meriem and baby Malika.

Today, Ruth continues to invest in this family's life, teaching Meriem how to bathe Malika and accompanying Meriem to Malika's first doctor's appointment. Meriem and Ahmed refer to Ruth as "Grandma," and they always welcome her with hugs and kisses. Ruth is likely the first Christian Ahmed and Meriem have ever known.

Ruth is doing exactly what God calls us to do—love others, do good, be rich in good works, and be generous. She is generous with her money, her time, and her love. What is remarkable about this relationship is that Ruth feels she is the one who is blessed. This is what results from lifestyle generosity. Both the receiver and the giver are richly blessed as God is pleased! Ruth is a beautiful example of living a generous life.

In addition to giving to our churches and charities, here are some creative ways of making generosity a part of our daily lives. Some cost money, and some don't. These actions will show our love for God by loving others, turn our focus away from ourselves, and allow us to experience and distribute joy along the way.

Lifestyle Generosity Ideas

- Pay for the meal of the person behind you in the fast-food drive-through.
- Pay for the movie tickets for the person in line behind you.
- Give a pair of concert or game tickets to a stranger.
- Tape the amount needed for a snack or drink to a vending machine.
- Tip your restaurant server a huge amount.
- Thank the cooks personally.
- Leave a note of thanks with your tip.
- Compliment a stranger.
- Send donuts or a pizza to a construction site.
- Leave a treat for your mail carrier.
- Offer the FedEx or UPS delivery person something to drink.
- Pull bags off the airport conveyor belt for those who could use help.
- Give up your seat on a crowded bus or train.
- Bring flowers to your coworkers.
- Take your employees on a mission trip that you pay for.

- Write notes of appreciation to your children's/ grandchildren's teachers.

- Bring biscuits or donuts to teachers when you drop off your kids at school.

- Take pictures of the other kids on your children's/ grandchildren's sports teams and distribute them.

- Use a disposable camera to take pictures at a party, and leave the camera with the host.

- Write a thank-you note to someone who has positively influenced your life.

- When a driver merges into your lane, greet him or her with a wave and a smile.

- Give another driver your parking spot.

- Return a shopping cart for someone loading a car.

- Let someone in front of you at the checkout line.

- Pick up flowers at the grocery store, and after you check out, give them to the cashier.

- Pray that God will give you more ideas on how to practice lifestyle generosity!

CHAPTER 6

THE TRUTH ABOUT TAXES

O ther than the 1.7 million accountants and auditors in the United States, most people don't like taxes. Take a look at all the different taxes we pay.

- Individual federal income taxes

- Individual state income taxes

- Federal and state social insurance taxes (e.g., Social Security, Medicare, Medicaid, unemployment)

- Federal excise taxes (e.g., gasoline tax, aviation tax, tobacco tax)

- State sales and excise taxes (e.g., sales tax, gasoline tax)

- Property taxes (real estate tax, personal property tax)

- Federal and state corporate income taxes

- Estate, inheritance, and gift taxes

- Local taxes (e.g., income tax, sales tax, automobile tax)

According to the Tax Foundation, Americans spend more in a year on taxes than on food, clothing, and housing combined.[35] This same group proclaims Tax Freedom Day each year, the day when enough money has been earned to pay all the taxes owed for the year. In 2013 Tax Freedom Day was April 18, meaning Americans worked 108 days just to accumulate the funds needed to pay their taxes. This equates to 29.4 percent of all the income our country earns in twelve months being paid in some form of tax.[36]

Many Christians are increasingly frustrated with the taxes the government imposes, especially as more and more of the money we work for is used for programs and policies we often disagree with. But as much as we complain about taxes today, they used to be more formidable, at least for those with the highest incomes. During the 1950s and 1960s, the top income tax bracket paid 90 percent of what they earned! As recently as 1981, married couples sent 70 percent of their income above $215,400 to the federal government.[37]

While our taxes aren't this steep today, they are not likely to decrease anytime soon, since the federal government and most state governments are in serious debt. It is frustrating when we don't end up with as much money as we could have had.

This is the same reaction we see by those in Philippi in Acts 16. Initially, Paul and Silas were permitted to preach the gospel openly in this city with no repercussions. However, when Paul cast out the demon from the fortune-telling slave girl who was making a lot of money for her owners, he and Silas were seized, beaten, and thrown into prison. It was as if the unbelieving citizens said, "Once you start messing with our money, you have gone too far" (Acts 16:16–23).

Similar to the slave girl's owners, we get angry when the government takes more of our money. And that reveals a big part of the problem; we consider it *our* money. When we recognize that God owns it all, our financial perspective changes, and we begin to view government and taxes differently.

We Are Subject to Governmental Authority

> Every person is to be in subjection to the governing authorities. For there is no authority except from God, and those which exist are established by God. Therefore whoever resists authority has opposed the ordinance of God; and they who have opposed will receive condemnation upon themselves. (Rom. 13:1–2 NASB)

What was once a nation under God is now full of courts interpreting laws to remove prayer from schools, ban the Ten Commandments from government buildings, and remove nativity scenes from public places. Although many of us are often discouraged by the direction of our country, what should concern us more is that bitterness and resentfulness toward the government could distract us from hearing God's calling and possibly bring condemnation upon ourselves.

While we are not required to endorse poor government decisions or approve of wastefulness, according to Romans 13, we are to subject ourselves to the governing authorities, because God appoints all leadership. God expects us to abide by established laws, unless those requirements explicitly conflict with the Bible.

Max Lucado greatly challenged believers' view of the government with his powerful statement on Election Day, November 6, 2012.

> Let others lose sleep over the election. Let others grow bitter from party or petty rivalries. Let others cast their hope with the people of the elephant or the donkey. Not followers of Jesus. We place our trust in the work of God. How many kings has He seen come and go? How many nations has He

seen stand and fall? He is above them all. And He oversees them all. So, while others get anxious, we don't. Here is what we do: we pray.

> *First of all, that petitions, prayers, intercession and thanksgiving be made for all people—for kings and all those in authority, that we may live peaceful and quiet lives in all godliness and holiness. This is good, and pleases God our Savior, who wants all people to be saved and to come to a knowledge of the truth (1 Timothy 2:1–4 NIV).*

It is time to take this job seriously. Over the next hours and days ahead, turn your heart toward heaven and ask God to:

- Unite our country
- Strengthen us
- Appoint and anoint our next president[38]

Christians Must Pay the Taxes They Owe

> Render to all what is due them: tax to whom tax is due; custom to whom custom; fear to whom fear; honor to whom honor. (Rom. 13:7 NASB)

If we owe it, we must pay it. This verse does not say we should pay tax only to those who use it wisely, or only to those who are godly. It says to pay what we owe.

> And He said to them, "Then render to Caesar the things that are Caesar's, and to God the things that are God's." (Luke 20:25 NASB)

Caesar was not a godly man, and he ruled his empire with an iron fist. Yet Christ taught that taxes were indeed to be paid to this dictator.

Matthew 17 provides additional insight into Jesus' instruction about paying taxes.

> When they had come to Capernaum, those who collected the two-drachma tax came to Peter, and said, "Does your teacher not pay the two-drachma tax?" He said, "Yes." And when he came into the house, Jesus spoke to him first, saying, "What do you think, Simon? From whom do the kings of the earth collect customs or poll-tax, from their sons or from strangers?" And upon his saying, "From strangers," Jesus said to him, "Then the sons are exempt. However, so that we do not offend them, go to the sea and throw in a hook, and take the first fish that comes up; and when you open its mouth, you will find a shekel. Take that and give it to them for you and Me." (Matt. 17:24–27 NASB)

I love this story! Can you imagine the looks on the faces of the temple tax collectors when Peter caught the fish and took the exact amount needed to settle their taxes from its mouth? While this was a temple tax and not a government tax, we can transfer the principle Jesus creatively demonstrated to our own taxes. Paying this tax allowed Him to stay above reproach, protect His witness, and prevent taxes from becoming a distraction.

As we saw in chapter 5, God tells us to do our giving first. Paying taxes is second in the priority order of spending.

The Truth about Taxes ...
Taxes Are Not the Problem

The truth is that taxes are not the problem. Blaming our financial struggles on taxes reveals an issue with our perspective. Are we forgetting that God owns it all? Do we believe life consists of our possessions? Do we think lower taxes would make our lives better, because we would have more to spend on what we want? Do we really suppose having more money will make our lives better? When we blame taxes, we stoke our appetites to desire more money, which creates serious consequences.

> But those who want to get rich fall into temptation and a snare and many foolish and harmful desires which plunge men into ruin and destruction. (1 Tim. 6:9 NASB)

If we see taxes as the government taking what rightfully belongs to us, we will be bitter, angry, and resentful. But if we understand that God owns all of our money and establishes authority, we will be more likely to submit to the government and realize paying taxes is a necessary and important priority.

Seek Wise Tax Counsel

The *CCH Standard Federal Tax Reporter* needed over 73,000 pages to print the Federal Tax Code for 2012. For most of us, this complexity makes it impossible to accurately prepare our own tax returns. We need help.

> The way of a fool is right in his own eyes, but a wise man is he who listens to counsel. (Prov. 12:15 NASB)

While we have to pay the taxes we rightfully owe, we do not have to pay more than we owe. The coins Peter pulled from the mouth of the fish equaled the exact amount owed, not a fraction more. What kind of counsel should we seek to help us with our tax planning? Wise counsel.

> He who walks with wise men will be wise, but the companion of fools will suffer harm. (Prov. 13:20 NASB)

Wisdom is the application of knowledge in a practical and successful way. Wisdom requires knowledge, which in this case is technical in nature, because it deals with the tax code. Secondly, it is acting prudently with that knowledge, which requires insight from God. James states that all wisdom comes from God and that He gives it freely to those who ask. When seeking financial advice, partner with someone who has both technical expertise and godly insight in order to receive wise counsel.

General Tax Planning Tips

Flee from Tax Advice That Is Dishonest

Proverbs 13:20 does not say that the companion of fools will become a fool; it says that he will suffer harm.

Be Careful of Making a Decision Primarily to Save on Taxes

Allow the tax effect to be one part of the process rather than the primary motivation.

Strive for Simple Tax Planning

Never participate in a strategy you do not understand.

> O LORD, my heart is not proud, nor my eyes haughty; nor do I involve myself in great matters, or in things too difficult for me. (Ps. 131:1 NASB)

If you cannot explain a tax strategy to your spouse, pass on it.

Be Proactive in Tax Planning

The value of forward tax planning is often a matter of timing. Imagine receiving a phone call from your tax preparer on April 15, explaining you owe an unexpected $15,000 to the IRS today. Assume conversely that you work with your financial planner in July to formulate a tax projection for the current year. It reveals you will owe $15,000 next April. While the news is the same, you handle it much better. Why? You have nine months to prepare for the liability and possibly implement strategies to reduce the tax owed.

Be above Reproach with Taxes

As believers, we should be completely honest, without even a hint of immorality.

> But immorality or any impurity or greed must not even be named among you, as is proper among saints; (Eph. 5:3 NASB)

> He who is faithful in a very little thing is faithful also in much; and he who is unrighteous in a very little thing is unrighteous also in much. (Luke 16:10 NASB)

> Wealth obtained by fraud dwindles, but the one who gathers by labor increases it. (Prov. 13:11 NASB)

Two Strategies to Make Tax Planning More Effective and Efficient

Give Appreciated Assets to Charity

The ways to legally avoid paying income taxes are quite limited. But donating long-term appreciated property to charity is one technique that actually uses the government to fund part of your charitable giving.

Assume you want to donate $10,000 to your church. Typically, you would give cash. But let's say you bought a stock five years ago for $2,000 that is now worth $10,000. You should consider gifting these shares in-kind to your church instead of cash. By doing so, you avoid paying the capital gains taxes that would otherwise be owed on the $8,000 profit when the stock is sold.

Because the church is a qualified nonprofit, it does not pay any tax after selling the investment. You receive a charitable deduction in the amount of the stock's value on the date it is given to the church ($10,000 in our example). You can now use the $10,000 of cash you were going to give to your church to put back into your investment account to replace the gift of stock.

If you desire, you can even buy back that same stock. The investment you purchase with the cash now has a basis of $10,000 instead of $2,000, meaning that the government has paid for the tax on the $8,000 gain.

It is important to only gift appreciated property that you have held for at least one year and that is not part of a retirement account.

Donor-Advised Funds (DAF)

A donor-advised fund is a charitable giving account you establish to consolidate and simplify your charitable giving. You make tax-deductible gifts of cash and/or appreciated assets to your account and then recommend grant distributions to the charities of your choice. It is essentially a way to create your own low-cost foundation.

One of the most popular DAFs is the National Christian Foundation (NCF), which is the largest Christian grant-making foundation in the world. Since 1982, NCF has received over $5 billion in contributions and made over $3.5 billion in grants to thousands of churches, ministries, and nonprofits. Headquartered in Atlanta, they now have over twenty-five affiliate offices around the country.

Here are some reasons to consider a donor-advised fund with the National Christian Foundation.

- Only one receipt is needed for all gifts made to your DAF, even though your grants may be distributed to multiple charities. This is important, since the IRS now requires detailed receipts for all charitable giving dated before your tax return is filed. Charitable giving audits are becoming much more common. Using a DAF for all your charitable giving makes it easy to satisfy this documentation requirement.

- Gifts of appreciated investments are easily handled and distributed by DAFs like NCF.

- It is possible to make gifts of appreciated real estate or certain closely held business interests to NCF. One of our firm's clients recently gave 10 percent of his closely owned business to NCF before selling. This allowed the business owner to leverage the amount of money he wanted to give to charity from the sale, since he did not have to pay capital gains taxes on the 10 percent given to NCF.

- Grants to charities can be recommended at your discretion, or you can request automatic distributions to occur at specific intervals.

- The charitable deduction is credited in the year your DAF receives the contribution, even if the grants to charities are made in a later year. This is a wonderful strategy for someone who may want to prefund future giving due to changes in income or tax laws.

- NCF has a low cost structure of 1/365th of 1 percent per

day, or 1 percent each year (with a minimum fee of $10/month). Many gifts to NCF are quickly distributed to charity, making the costs minimal.

- NCF possesses the ability to handle charitable gift annuities, charitable remainder trusts, and charitable lead trusts.

- The NCF Dashboard helps manage and track your giving by categorizing your charitable gifts and tabulating your giving history over various time periods.

- NCF provides several investment options for assets in your giving fund that will not be immediately directed to charities.

- NCF allows you to make anonymous gifts to charity and still claim an income tax deduction.

For more information on the National Christian Foundation, visit *www.nationalchristian.com.*

Consult a tax professional before implementing any of the tax strategies discussed in this chapter.

Chapter 7

Free from Debt

The way society views debt has changed dramatically over the past few generations, as the late Lewis Grizzard creatively described in the *Atlanta Journal & Constitution*.

> Donald Trump owes 3 billion dollars. I read that in the papers. Trump, in an incredibly excessive way, is merely an example of how my generation looks at money in comparison to the way our parents did. If my mother had been put in charge of the nation's budget, there never would have been a deficit.
>
> A friend of my age said, "My father was proudest of the fact everything he owned was paid for." I used to tell him, "But you don't have very much." He would always say, "But what little I have nobody can take away." Can you say that? I couldn't.

I worked with a guy who was telling me about a letter he got from one of his creditors. "They're mad about the fact I missed a payment," he said. "The way I pay for my bills is I put them all in a hat. Then, I reach into the hat without looking and pull out a bill. I keep doing that until I'm out of money. There are always a few bills left in the hat, but at least everybody I owe has the same chance of being pulled out of the hat. I wrote the people back and told them if they sent me another nasty letter, I wouldn't even put them in the hat anymore!"

Haven't we all been guilty of our own little episodes of extravagance and greed? Our frugal, save-for-a-rainy-day parents said things like, "Never borrow from Peter to pay Paul." The Debt Generation sports bumper stickers that say, "He who dies with the most toys wins." That's sad.[39]

Fortunately, we have seen personal debt levels decline a bit in the past few years. Part of this is due to the more restrictive standards of lenders. It has also helped that Dave Ramsey and others have exposed the dangers of debt and encouraged many to reduce and eliminate their liabilities. But debt is still a significant issue for families and our country.

Debt is an obligation to pay something owed to another. Types of liabilities include home mortgages, equity loans, auto loans, unsecured loans, credit cards, even utility and phone bills. Any product or service we use or consume *before* paying for it constitutes a debt. This is broader than our typical definition and is important to realize as we discover what the Bible says about owing money.

Before taking on debt, we should evaluate it three ways—biblically, emotionally, and financially.

Biblical Considerations of Debt

As we discussed in previous chapters, God cares about how we handle money. Richard Halverson says,

> Jesus Christ said more about money than about any other single thing because, when it comes to a man's real nature, money is of first importance. Money is an exact index to a man's true character. All through Scripture there is an intimate correlation between the development of a man's character and how he handles money.[40]

While the Bible does not specifically prohibit Christians from taking on debt, Scripture does include many verses full of cautions and warnings. In fact, in the Old Testament, being debt-free was considered a reward (Deut. 28:1–2, 12), while being saddled with liabilities was one of the punishments for disobedience (Deut. 28:15, 43–44).

Christians Must Pay Their Debts

> The wicked borrows and does not pay back, but the righteous is gracious and gives. (Ps. 37:21 NASB)

> When you make a vow to God, do not be late in paying it, for He takes no delight in fools. Pay what you vow! It is better that you should not vow than that you should vow and not pay. (Ecc. 5:4–5 NASB)

Before acquiring debt, we need a reasonable plan of repayment, remembering that paying our liabilities is a higher priority than savings, investments, and living expenses. When we take on debt haphazardly, we assume the future will be stable and prosperous. But what if it is not? House values could plummet and make it impossible to sell or refinance. We might spend an expected bonus that never materializes or make a bad investment with borrowed money. In 2012 over 1.2 million individuals filed for personal bankruptcy because they could not pay their debts.[41] The truth is that most people in dire financial circumstances are there because of the excessive amount they owe.

Avoid Cosigning a Loan

The act of cosigning, also called surety, makes you responsible for another's obligations.

> He who is guarantor for a stranger will surely suffer for it, but he who hates being a guarantor is secure. (Prov. 11:15 NASB)

> A man lacking in sense pledges, and becomes guarantor in the presence of his neighbor. (Prov. 17:18 NASB)

The Bible is clear that it is not wise to cosign for others. When a lender requires a guarantor, he or she determined the risk is too great to justify the potential profit without this extra protection. Since 50 percent of all cosigners end up paying back part or all of another person's debt, this biblical principle provides protection.[42]

There are situations where it seems legitimate to cosign for a friend or family member. Maybe your child needs help buying his first home or a good friend needs assistance securing a business loan. Consider these better options.

Make a Loan

Instead of cosigning, think about making a personal loan. While loans are permissible in Scripture, they still come with some words of caution, since relationships are always more important than money. Relationships often suffer when payments are not made or when the parties involved feel they are not being treated fairly. It is better to suffer financial loss than to live in conflict with a believer or to bring a dispute before unbelievers (1 Cor. 6:1–7).

If you choose to extend a personal loan, you need to understand some important IRS rules. In general, a fair market interest rate (as determined by IRS applicable federal rates) must be charged, and the lender is required to pay taxes on that interest. If a lower interest rate is used, you are still required to pay taxes on the higher interest that should have been applied. This is called imputed interest.

Fortunately, a few important exceptions to these imputed interest rules exist. If the loan is for less than $10,000 and for non-income producing property, the imputed interest requirements do not apply. In addition, these rules do not apply when the loan is for $100,000 or less, and the borrower has less than $1,000 of net investment income for the year. In both circumstances, it is permissible to charge an interest rate of 0 percent without paying taxes on the imputed interest. Avoiding imputed interest can have obvious benefits for the borrower and is consistent with Old Testament verses that discourage Christians from charging interest to other believers.

Agreed-upon loan terms should always be documented in writing. Make sure to consult a tax professional for your specific situation, and always proceed with caution before making a personal loan. Jesus goes so far as to tell us to not expect repayment when we lend (Luke 6:34, 35), which brings us to the second option to consider instead of cosigning.

Make a Gift

When a friend or family member is in need, making a gift is often the best solution. A gift can be of great help to the receiver and almost always preserves the relationship.

Be aware of gifting regulations, because the IRS actually limits how much one person can give to another in a calendar year without facing gift tax consequences. In 2013 that limit is $14,000 per person. This means a married couple can give another married couple up to $56,000 in any one year, as both husband and wife can give $14,000 to the receiving husband and wife.

It is possible to combine a loan and a gift and forgive part of the loan each year, up to the limits of the annual gift exclusion. For example, if $100,000 is needed by the recipient, a loan can be structured (possibly for 0 percent interest based on the imputed interest rules) for $100,000. If desired, the entire loan can be forgiven over a few years by using the $14,000 annual gift exclusion.

Regardless of the situation you face, remember to pray and seek wise counsel before making a loan or gift.

Don't Borrow to Invest

> A faithful man will abound with blessings, but he who makes haste to be rich will not go unpunished. A man with an evil eye hastens after wealth, and does not know that want will come upon him. (Prov. 28:20, 22 NASB)

> But those who want to get rich fall into temptation and a snare and many foolish and harmful desires which plunge men into ruin and destruction. (1 Tim. 6:9 NASB)

Investing with debt is usually the result of desiring to be rich. This principle cuts to the heart by examining our motivation. While we do have the possibility to make a greater profit when we borrow to invest, our ultimate financial objective is *not* to make as much money as we can. Our goal is to be faithful. Because the desire to be rich distorts our judgments and compromises our priorities, the warnings in Scripture are both stern and serious.

Be Willing to Wait

> Rest in the LORD and wait patiently for Him; do not fret because of him who prospers in his way, because of the man who carries out wicked schemes. Wait for the LORD, and keep His way, and He will exalt you to inherit the land; when the wicked are cut off, you will see it. (Ps. 37:7, 34 NASB)

> But the fruit of the Spirit is love, joy, peace, patience, kindness, goodness, faithfulness, (Gal. 5:22 NASB)

When our boys were young, we gave them a monthly allowance. One Saturday, Griffin asked me if it was time for his money. It was still a few days from the end of the month, so I told him he had to wait. There was a toy Griffin wanted to buy right away, not next week.

Being pretty determined, he reasoned, "Why don't you give me the money now. Then you don't have to pay me my allowance later."

I replied, "It does not work that way."

"Why not?" Griffin asked.

I said, "Because that would be debt."

Griffin shot back, "Yes, that's what I want. I want debt!"

We acquire debt because we are impatient and want stuff before we can completely pay for it. We live in an instant culture that does not like to wait for anything. It was good for Griffin to delay his gratification, even though he wanted the toy immediately. If we can learn to be patient with our consumptive desires, we learn an important spiritual discipline, a fruit of the Holy Spirit.

> You too be patient; strengthen your hearts, for the coming of the Lord is near. (Jas. 5:8 NASB)

Emotional Considerations of Debt

Debt Causes Stress

> The rich rules over the poor, and the borrower becomes the lender's slave. (Prov. 22:7 NASB)

It is stressful to owe money, and stress creates problems. According to a study by the Associated Press and AOL Health, stress from debt leads to a higher than average occurrence of health problems such as migraines, ulcers, and depression.[43] The ease of spending more than we have blurs wants and needs as we pursue the most recent trends, the latest electronic gadgets, a bigger house, or a new car. Credit card balances and monthly payments accumulate unnoticed until we realize we cannot pay all our bills. And as we spend, we certainly do not think about the stress and possible adverse health effects that can come from mounting debt.

Debt Creates Insecurity

> Owe nothing to anyone except to love one another;
> for he who loves his neighbor has fulfilled the law.
> (Rom. 13:8 NASB)

Remember when I divided my clients into two groups, the peace of mind group and the anxious group? In addition to being less generous, the worried bunch was characterized by having much more debt than their content counterparts. The fear of financial loss that accompanies debt is real.

Debt Reduces Freedom and Flexibility

In Scripture, a person was often ordered into slavery—the ultimate loss of freedom—because of debt.

> For this reason the kingdom of heaven may be compared to a king who wished to settle accounts

with his slaves. When he had begun to settle them, one who owed him ten thousand talents was brought to him. But since he did not have the means to repay, his lord commanded him to be sold, along with his wife and children and all that he had, and repayment to be made. (Matt. 18:23–25 NASB)

Now a certain woman of the wives of the sons of the prophets cried out to Elisha, "Your servant my husband is dead, and you know that your servant feared the LORD; and the creditor has come to take my two children to be his slaves. (2 Kings 4:1 NASB)

Although we don't experience these harsh consequences for unpaid debt today, loss of freedom and flexibility is still a reality. Several years ago, I worked with a client who had developed a very successful medical practice in a large North Carolina city. But he felt a strong calling from the Lord to move to the Appalachian Mountains to serve an impoverished community that lacked medical care. This move would mean a significant reduction in his income.

After exploring the details of a radical life change, he realized he was not going to be able to make this transition, because his current debt load was too great. While his substantial income easily covered his monthly payments, the problem came with the prospect of his income being reduced. The debt stole his freedom to follow the Lord's leading.

The mind of man plans his way, but the Lord directs his steps. (Prov. 16:9 NASB)

When our liability payments restrict us from responding to the Spirit's call, we are enslaved to debt. When our monthly payments stretch us so thin we cannot give generously, we are enslaved to debt. Create a financial situation that makes it easy to follow the Lord's direction now and in the future. Less debt always equals more freedom and flexibility.

Financial Considerations of Debt

No Good Deals with Debt

Debt almost always guarantees you will pay more than the actual cost of an item. It is the opposite of getting a good deal. We lose sight of the total cost when we are conditioned to think in terms of a monthly payment. Automobile dealers understand this when they only promote the monthly payments required for a vehicle purchase or lease.

A $35,000 automobile comes with a monthly payment of $677 when financed at 6 percent over five years. This brings the total that will be paid to $40,599, an increase of 16 percent over the original sales price.

On a bigger scale, a $400,000 home mortgage with a 4 percent interest over thirty years creates a total cost of $687,478, a whopping 72 percent more than the price of the home! On the other hand, paying an extra $350/month removes almost eight years from the thirty-year loan and saves $82,000 in interest.

Paying Off Debt Is a Risk-Free Investment Return

When we make extra payments of principal or pay off a debt entirely, we are giving ourselves a guaranteed return in the amount of the interest rate. Take that $400,000 home mortgage at 4 percent, for example. Paying that off is the equivalent of getting a risk-free investment return.

This is excellent, since there are no other investments completely without risk. The least risky investments are savings and money-market accounts, CDs, and Treasuries. As of the writing of this chapter, savings and money-market accounts are paying less than 0.5 percent/year in interest. A five-year jumbo

CD is under 2 percent/year and a thirty-year Treasury bond has an annual yield below 3 percent. That guaranteed return of 4 percent looks pretty good! For higher-interest liabilities, the financial argument for retiring debt is even more convincing.

The Value of What Is Purchased with Debt Should Exceed the Cost of Financing

This principle is twofold. First, the value of the item purchased should always be greater than the debt balance. If not, the loan is classified as being upside-down (owing more than the item is worth). Second, the item purchased with debt should appreciate at a rate greater than the interest rate. Thus, as a general rule of good financial sense, do not go into debt for items that decrease in value.

Cars depreciate in value. Therefore, it is wise to pay cash for vehicles. This is not always easy, as I found out early in my working career. I needed a car before we had saved very much money. In fact, I had less than $1,000 to spend on an automobile. Susan and I really wanted to pay cash, so we searched for the best car we could pay for. The winner turned out to be a Honda Accord with over 200,000 miles and an air conditioner that only occasionally worked. But it was a great car that served me well for over two years. We actually sold that car at a garage sale for just $100 less than we paid for it! By then, we had saved enough to pay cash for a nicer vehicle.

In addition to cars, almost all credit card purchases are for items that depreciate. So do not carry balances on credit cards.

Items that increase in value can be considered for financing from a financial perspective, but they still need to be evaluated spiritually and emotionally before proceeding. Houses are an example of items that *should* appreciate. However, it is no longer a certainty that a home's value will rise at a level that equals or exceeds the interest rate. So even with our home mortgages, our goal should be to pay these off as quickly as possible.

Questions to Ask before Taking on Debt

Biblical

- Do we have the freedom before God to take on this debt?
- Will the debt interfere with our ability to give and be generous?
- What is our motivation for taking on the debt?
- Will it be more difficult to serve God with this debt?
- Are there any options available other than debt?

Emotional

- Will this debt create stress or anxiety?
- Will this debt reduce flexibility?
- Do my spouse and I agree on the debt?
- Can our goals be achieved in any way other than this debt?

Financial

- Will the value of the item purchased with debt always be greater than the remaining debt balance?
- Will this debt place an excessive strain on our budget?
- Will this debt interfere with other, more important financial goals?

Steps to Getting Out of Debt

Pray

> Be anxious for nothing, but in everything by prayer and supplication with thanksgiving let your requests be made known to God. (Phil. 4:6 NASB)

Acknowledge your financial position before God, and ask for His guidance and wisdom.

Determine Where You Are

You must know where you are in order to develop a plan to get out of debt. Begin by writing down all your debts, noting the interest rates, monthly payments, and lengths of term.

Stop Going into Debt

It does not do any good to reduce debt if we replace it with new debt. The goal is to become totally debt-free as soon as possible, and this will only happen if we stop going into debt.

Listen to how a professional organizer remembers her early days. "When I first started as an organizing consultant and was faced with a huge backlog of client's papers, I mistakenly thought I needed to eliminate the backlog first, and then move on to develop an orderly new system. I quickly learned that it's a waste of time and energy to feel guilty over yesterday's pileups—you've got to start with today's and plan for tomorrow."[44]

The same is true with debt. The first step is to stop taking on new debt. Spend less than you earn each year, and save for upcoming major purchases and emergencies by accumulating three to six months of living expenses in a money-market account. Without this savings, you will be forced to take on debt to pay for those unexpected expenses that seem to occur every year. In addition to your emergency fund, you also need to save for upcoming major purchases that don't fit in your normal budget.

Snowball Theory of Debt Repayment

This debt-elimination strategy has been around for years, but it recently gained more attention as Dave Ramsey promoted it. The debt snowball steps are as follows.

- List all debts in order, from smallest balance to largest.

- Pay the minimum payment on every debt, except for the one with the smallest debt balance.

- Contribute as much extra as possible to the monthly payment on this smallest debt until it is paid off.

- Once the smallest debt is paid in full, you have freed up the amount of the minimum payment on the smallest debt balance, plus the amount of the extra payments you were making. Take both amounts and apply them as additional payments on the second-smallest debt balance.

- Once the second-smallest debt is retired, you have the payments from the first debt, the second debt, and the extra payments that can all be added to the third-smallest debt balance. The amount of your total payments continues to grow with each debt that is paid off, hence the name of "snowball."

- Continue to follow this strategy until all your debts are retired and you are debt-free.

The debt snowball works from both a financial and an emotional standpoint. By attacking the smallest debt first, you are motivated as you eliminate one debt and are able to pay even more toward the next debt. The key is to get the snowball rolling!

I recently met with a young dentist with $271,000 in various school loans. By making substantial extra payments of principal each month, and employing the snowball theory of debt repayment, we were able to construct a plan for him to be completely free from all of his debt in fewer than four years!

Once all of your debt is retired,
keep making the payments … to yourself

Remember to keep rolling your debt payments forward until all your liabilities are retired. Once you are debt-free, keep making your monthly payments, but make them to yourself. This gives you a substantial amount of extra funds that can be used for savings, investing, or even additional giving. Although you could spend more since you no longer have debt payments, you will improve your ability to be financially free by keeping your lifestyle at the same level and using these monthly payments to accomplish other goals.

Easier Said Than Done

Some things are much easier said than done. I remember when Keaton was playing Little League baseball as a twelve-year-old, just a couple years ago. When he was up to bat, it was clear he was afraid of getting hit by the ball. As the pitcher released the ball, Keaton moved his feet away from the plate.

After one of his games I said, "Don't be afraid of the ball when you are hitting. You can't be a good hitter if you are afraid."

He replied, "You can't just say, 'Don't be afraid,' and I won't be afraid. It is not that easy. I am petrified. Do you know how much it will hurt if I get hit? Have you seen the size of some of these pitchers?"

He made a good point. It is kind of like that with debt. We really can't just say, "Don't ever take on debt." It is almost impossible to not take on debt, especially if we define debt correctly and realize we use a lot of services before we actually pay for them (utilities, phone, etc.). But it is hard to have a healthy financial situation when we have a lot of liabilities.

So be careful.

Scripture does not say you can't ever borrow. It just says there are a lot of dangers with debt. So minimize it wherever possible, work hard to reduce it, and don't let it get out of control. And most of all, pay what you owe.

By the way, Keaton retired from baseball after his twelve-year-old season. It just was not worth the risk and stress. And for many of us, this is true about our debt. It is just too risky and distracting. Make a plan today to reduce and eliminate debt!

CHAPTER 8

INVESTING FOR THE FUTURE

In late 1999, we received a family gift to use for the future college educations of our three boys. I was excited and began to research how to invest the cash, eventually settling on several well-diversified mutual funds. They increased in value a little, but nothing happened fast, and I became impatient. I decided to take some of the money and buy an individual stock to see if we could make some real progress.

I stumbled on a small, growing company called PolyMedica, a supplier of diabetes home-testing kits. Knowing diabetes was a growing problem, projected to only get worse, this company seemed like a good buy. I invested a few thousand dollars into PolyMedica in each of the boy's accounts.

Now this was exciting. Almost every day when I checked the Internet, there seemed to be some kind of news about the company, and the stock was moving. It was really fun to watch the action and try to figure out why the price reacted like it did. Then, after about a week, the stock dropped 15 percent. I felt sick to my stomach and thought, *What a stupid investment that was.* Not quite yet ready to admit failure, I surmised that if it was a good buy last week, it was an even a better deal now. So I bought more. The following week, the stock started to climb, and by the third week, it had made up all the loss and zoomed past my original purchase price. I was thrilled and thought, *What a great decision it was to buy PolyMedica!*

As the stock continued to rise, I wanted to own even more PolyMedica. So I started selling my mutual funds to buy additional shares. I began each workday researching PolyMedica. I learned that when there was an asterisk by the stock symbol, it meant there was a new story for the company, and it seemed to always be good. I continued to buy more and more as the stock price rose. Before long, almost the entire portfolio for each boy was invested in PolyMedica. I had not shared any of this with Susan, deciding it was probably best to keep it to myself for now. I would let her know about my brilliance once I had made a lot of money for our boys.

I estimated my average buying price was around $25/share, and PolyMedica was now trading in the $35 range. I loved looking at the total amount in each account and seeing how it was growing. Keep in mind, this was the year 2000, and the rest of the US stock market was in the beginning stages of a significant three-year decline. The NASDAQ market was already in a complete sell-off, yet PolyMedica (a NASDAQ stock) seemed to do nothing but increase.

Having no more money to buy additional shares, my days became filled with constant monitoring of ticker symbol PLMD. My days were good when the price was up, and I was in a sour mood when it declined. It was not unusual to see the total balance of the three accounts swing by $5,000 or more in just a day or two. Monitoring PLMD became quite addicting and distracting. I found myself constantly thinking about this small Massachusetts company, which I had never heard of just a few months before.

Then something really amazing happened. PolyMedica released its third-quarter earnings report for 2000, a date that had been circled on my calendar for weeks. It blew away all the analysts' projections. It was official; PolyMedica was a runaway growth machine. More and more investors started to take notice, and the stock price shot up like never before, surging above $50/share! I could not believe it. In less than a year, I had doubled our gift money in the midst of a horrible stock market. I began to swell with pride. At the same time, I began to fear I'd lose what I had gained. The anxiety was exhausting. But it would be ridiculous to sell a stock that did nothing but increase.

Right?

As November approached, I decided it was time to share the good news with Susan. Because of her husband's amazing skill, our three boys would indeed be able to go to college. I shared the whole story about PolyMedica with her, emphasizing how well the stock I found had performed. And then I told her how much the accounts were worth. As I was waiting for her adoring response and proclamation of how well she had married, I was met with a completely unanticipated reply.

In a somewhat shaking voice she said, "Sell it." Thinking she had misunderstood, I reiterated how we (I thought this was a good time to include her on this) had made a ton of money.

Again she said, "I think you should sell it."

"Why in the world should we sell it?" I shot back.

She replied, "What if it goes down? It makes me really nervous to have so much in one stock."

Clearly she did not realize this was PolyMedica that we were talking about. It does not go down; it only goes up! Plus, what does she know about this company that I had studied inside and out for almost a year.

Our conversation ended, but I could not stop thinking about her response. I vacillated between being angry and wondering if she was right. And I did not like the tension the discussion had created. As I continued to reflect, I started to comprehend how nice it would be to sell and not think about PLMD anymore. We would make a great profit and be done. Of course, I would have to find something else to invest in, but I could do that.

I went back to Susan with a plan. "Babe, I think you may be right and that we should sell PolyMedica. But let's wait until it hits $60/share. It is at $57/share right now, and the way this stock performs, it will probably hit $60 in the next few days."

She seemed relieved and said, "I will just feel a lot better when it is sold."

With that as my plan, I entered limit orders to sell all of PLMD at $60/share. What a run it had been! I never dreamed I could make so much money in such a short period of time, especially in the midst of such a difficult stock market.

I continued to watch PolyMedica like a hawk. It always jumped around a good bit, so I was not too concerned when it dropped a few points. All the news continued to be positive. It got as high as $59/share in the next couple of weeks. On Friday, November 17, PolyMedica closed at $54/share. I remember thinking it would not be long before it hit $60.

As was my custom every trading day, my first order of business at eight o'clock on the next Monday morning was to pull up PLMD and see if there was any news from the weekend. On seeing the asterisk, I thought, *This is it. There is going to be some great news about PolyMedica that will send the stock to $60.*

As I clicked on the link next to the asterisk, I learned *Barron's* had published an article over the weekend about PolyMedica. To this day, I can remember my exact feeling as I read the headline, "FBI Investigates PolyMedica."

I was nauseated and started to shake. How could this be happening? I had already decided to sell. The order had been placed. It was supposed to hit $60, be sold, and we would live happily ever after. As I read the article, it only got worse. Apparently there were some serious questions about the company's marketing tactics and inappropriate Medicare charges, all of which PolyMedica would strongly deny later that day. This was not good. Not good at all!

What would happen to the stock price when the markets opened in ninety minutes? I watched every minute of the clock, anxiously waiting for 9:30. Additional news stories about PolyMedica popped up as the *Barron's* article became more widely read.

Finally, the markets opened. To my complete dismay, PLMD opened at $25.75/share on the morning of November 20, 2000. I was in shock. All my profits had been wiped out as the result of one magazine article. I called Susan to report the stunning and humiliating news. We decided to go ahead and sell it right away; the stress was all-consuming. So I sold PolyMedica at $25, exactly what my average buying price was.

I have thought a lot about PolyMedica in the years since then. It is not often that one investment serves as an example of violating almost every biblical principle that applies to investing. But my handling of PLMD did just that.

Let's take a look.

Poor Reasons to Save and Invest

Greed

I admit it. I was greedy. I wanted to get rich fast. I bought an individual stock because my mutual funds were not making enough money.

The character Gordon Gekko is famous for these words in the 1987 motion picture *Wall Street*.

> Greed, for lack of a better word, is good. Greed is right. Greed works. Greed clarifies, cuts through, and captures, the essence of the evolutionary spirit. Greed, in all of its forms; greed for life, for money, for love, knowledge, has marked the upward surge

of mankind and greed, you mark my words, will …
[save] that … malfunctioning corporation called
the U.S.A.[45]

Gekko reflects our craving to chase after more. But Scripture's description of greed is not at all glamorous.

> Then He said to them, "Beware, and be on your
> guard against every form of greed; for not even
> when one has an abundance does his life consist
> of his possessions." (Luke 12:15 NASB)

> But those who want to get rich fall into temptation
> and a snare and many foolish and harmful desires
> which plunge men into ruin and destruction. (1
> Tim. 6:9 NASB)

The desire to be rich is insatiable and leads to ruin. Greed clouds our judgment and must be avoided as a primary investment motivator.

Pride

When I told Susan how much money I made due to my careful research and skill to uncover the perfect stock, I was proud, really proud! But Scripture warns against this danger.

> Everyone who is proud in heart is an abomination
> to the LORD; Assuredly, he will not be unpunished.
> (Prov. 16:5 NASB)

> Instruct those who are rich in this present world
> not to be conceited … (1 Tim. 6:17a NASB)

When our net worth increases due to our growing investments, we have a tendency to swell with self-admiration, looking to our wealth, instead of the Lord, as our security and problem solver. King Solomon spoke of the self-sufficiency of the rich this way: "The wealth of the rich is their fortified city; they imagine it an unscaleable wall" (Prov. 18:11).

Fear

My fear of losing what I had gained was consuming.

> Make sure that your character is free from love of money, being content with what you have; for he himself has said, "I will never desert you, nor will I ever forsake you," so that we can confidently say, "The Lord is my helper; I will not be afraid. What will man do to me?" (Heb. 13:5–6 NASB)

When it comes to money, we have many fears. Those who lack financial resources worry about not having enough. "What if we cannot afford college, lose our jobs, encounter a medical crisis, or don't have enough to retire?"

The fear is different but often stronger (as I found out with PLMD) for those with plenty of wealth. They agonize over losing what they have. "How would life change if our income is decreased, if we suffer a large loss with our investments, or can no longer afford the privileges and possibilities that come with having an abundance of money?"

As the markets move up and down, investors battle with two opposite fears: the fear of loss if we stay invested and the fear of missing out on gain if we try to time the movements of stocks and bonds. These conflicting emotions make it extremely difficult to make wise and rational investment decisions. As our fears are manifested, the anguish they bring distract us from our relationship with the Lord and others. And regardless of how well or how poorly our investments perform, being distracted from what matters most is the more significant consequence.

A Biblical Philosophy of Investing

Remember, all we have is the Lord's. We are called to be faithful stewards of what He has given us. Scripture teaches that investments are a tool we can use to advance God's kingdom. The investment result is not all that matters. The process is of extreme importance.

What are the biblical principles regarding wise and faithful investment decisions?

Have a Greater Purpose

My purpose for investing the kids' accounts was to make as much money as I could. On the surface, this seems like a legitimate and noble reason to invest. However, without a greater rationale for investing, we lose perspective and are easily influenced and distracted by our emotions. Developing a biblical purpose for saving and investing is the first step in making wise decisions. At Ronald Blue & Co., we believe investing helps people provide for their families, do good works, and be generous.

> Instruct those who are rich in this present world …
> to do good, to be rich in good deeds, and to be
> generous and ready to share, storing up for
> themselves the treasure of a good foundation for
> the future, so that they may take hold of that which
> is life indeed. (1 Tim. 6:17–19 NASB)

Find the Right Balance

This biblical investment rationale promotes balance. There are three ways to invest: too little (presumptuous), too much (hoarding), or just enough (prudent savings).

If we don't save enough, we are guilty of presuming on the future.

> Suppose one of you wants to build a tower. Won't
> you first sit down and estimate the cost to see if
> you have enough money to complete it? (Luke
> 14:28 NIV)

We are warned against hording in the parable of the rich farmer. Having more crops than he could store, he tore down his barns and built bigger storehouses for all his grain and goods. Feeling content and satisfied by having more than he needed for many years, the rich man told himself to relax, eat, drink, and be merry. But in Luke 12:20-21 Jesus said to the self-absorbed farmer, "Fool! Tonight your soul is required of you. And the things you have prepared, whose will they be? This is how it will be with anyone who stores up things for himself but is not rich toward God."

> I have seen a grievous evil under the sun: wealth
> hoarded to the harm of its owners. (Ecc. 5:13 NIV)

Our objective should be to strive for the middle ground. Let's call this *prudent savings*. To figure out where we fall in these three areas of savings likely requires financial planning and soul-searching. Our culture is obsessed with creating wealth. But as believers, we must consider the greater purpose for investing and the biblical principles that guide how we should invest.

How to Invest

Be Humble

If I had been willing to seek wise counsel rather than arrogantly thinking I could amass great wealth in that one perfect stock, I would have quickly seen the error of my ways with PolyMedica.

Wise investing requires humbly understanding we cannot know the future with certainty. Humility leads to better outcomes when we focus on the process of investing (why we invest and how we invest), rather than just short-term performance. Humility encourages us to seek wise counsel and to keep our hope in God, trusting Him for the outcomes He controls.

Understand Risk

Until my PolyMedica stock crashed, I never considered the possibility of losing so much so fast. I was fearful of losing 15 or 20 percent in a bad month. But I never thought I might lose over 50 percent in one day.

Investment growth requires risk. Consistent with the parable of the talents in Matthew 25, taking risk in an attempt to realize a return is reasonable. But, what is risk?

Most define risk as the probable range prices can shift up or down as defined by historical movements. Actually, risk is the possibility of loss associated with the prospect of growth; risk is linked to what causes or destroys growth. Greater opportunities for growth *always* come with higher levels of risk, so we must view these together. Investors cannot expect to receive a return that is not proportionate to its risk. Led by Wall Street in the 1980s and Silicon Valley in the 1990s, the investment community focused almost exclusively on return possibilities, with barely a glance toward risk. The market crash of 2008–2009 changed this oversight.

As investors, we continuously face a number of risks, including:

- Longevity risk—outliving our money
- Inflation risk—losing purchasing power as prices increase
- Volatility risk—having to sell assets when values are low
- Behavioral risk—making bad decisions based on fear or greed

We have to understand the risks involved with various investment options and then decide the appropriate amount of risk to take.

> There is a grievous evil which I have seen under the sun: riches being hoarded by their owner to his hurt. When those riches were lost through a bad investment and he had fathered a son, then there was nothing to support him. (Ecc. 5:13–14 NASB)

Risk must be proportionate to our needs. As the verses in Ecclesiastes 5 teach, taking excessive risk with assets needed for critical short-term needs is foolish. To accurately pair risk and return, investors must first determine when they will need their invested funds. Less risk should be taken for resources needed in the short term, while more risk can be assumed for longer-term needs. For amounts needed in fewer than ten years, it does not make sense to invest in aggressive investments that can incur steep losses that may take years to recover. We don't want to be forced to make withdrawals at depressed prices. This is why planning is so important to determine when our invested funds will be needed.

For most investors, their two greatest risks are catastrophic loss and inflation. Comparing returns to a friend or an index does nothing to help reach goals. Our tendency is toward coveting, which we must protect against. We have an entire financial industry and media that promotes coveting another's return. It is very dangerous to never be satisfied.

Goals are accomplished with real returns that preserve purchasing power in the future. If an index underperforms inflation (like the S&P 500 did for much of the decade of 2000–2010), your investments can beat the S&P 500 and still not help you reach your goals. Striving for real returns (returns above inflation) relate directly to preserving purchasing power and meeting long-term goals.

Practice Diversification

My lack of diversification in the kids' accounts was obvious; one stock does not equal variety. Diversification reflects humility, while concentration implies arrogance. Since we don't know the future, we need to diversify our investments. Solomon understood this need to mitigate risk.

> Divide your portion to seven, or even to eight, for you do not know what misfortune may occur on the earth. (Ecc. 11:2 NASB)

Living in Charlotte, I have worked with a number of executives over the years from Bank of America and Wachovia (now Wells Fargo). Inevitably, most of their wealth was concentrated in their institutions.

When I shared the principle of diversification with them, they would say, "But Roger, you don't understand. The only reason I have enough money to be a client is because of my employer. My wealth has come from my bank salary, my ownership of bank stock, my bank stock options, and my 401k that is invested in the bank's stock."

I would remind them that Scripture says, "Diversify, because you do not know what misfortune may occur on the earth."

These were some of the strongest banks in the country, so I had no reason to suspect anything but continued financial success in the future. However, I knew the wisdom from the Bible regarding diversification. I certainly had no idea that in March of 2009, Bank of America stock would hit a low price of $3.09, after reaching a high of $55.08 just twenty-eight months earlier. Or that Wachovia would drop below $2/share in September of 2008, after being worth as much as $60.04 in April 2006. My banker-clients were thrilled with the diversification they implemented before these misfortunes occurred!

Investments should be strategically diversified across asset classes, countries, companies, and industries to protect against catastrophic losses. This is not a random division, as the economic environment will dictate some areas of heavier concentrations and others to minimize or avoid. But the practice of diversification should never be ignored.

Plod Patiently

I was not patient, and I did not plod with my PolyMedica adventure. I wanted to get richer faster. The reality was that I had twelve years before my first child would go to college, so I had plenty of time to be patient. Patient investing understands it takes a long time to achieve higher returns. The constant, even monotonous act of plodding adds an active element to patience, such as investing month after month.

> Dishonest money dwindles away, but he who gathers money little by little makes it grow. (Prov. 13:11 NIV)

The opposite of patient plodding is the desire to get rich quick.

> A faithful man will abound with blessings, but he who makes haste to be rich will not go unpunished. (Prov. 28:20 NASB)

The level of our patience and our ability to make careful, wise decisions will affect our stamina to weather short-term market fluctuations. Be diligent by focusing on the more predictable factors that determine long-term results. Do not be swayed by the unpredictable short-term movements of markets.

> Whoever is patient has great understanding, but one who is quick-tempered displays folly. (Prov. 14:29 NIV)

Invest According to Time Frames

When we invest according to our time frames, we are more patient, and that helps us to handle risk prudently. Consider the biggest market decline since the Great Depression, from late 2007 until early 2009. Assume your investments are divided into three buckets—one for money needed in the next two years, one for funds needed in the next three to nine years, and one for assets not needed for ten or more years.

The first bucket (two-year money) is invested very conservatively (money-market accounts and very short-term bond accounts) and, thus, maintains most of its value during the downturn. You are easily able to access these funds when needed without suffering a significant loss.

The cash flow needed from your investments in years three through nine is invested in various bond funds. While these suffer some declines during this bear market, the losses are much less severe than stock losses. Less than two years after the downturn began, these investments have fully recovered, and when you begin to make any necessary withdrawals, the values are higher than they were in 2007.

The assets needed in ten or more years are invested aggressively in various stock and commodity funds, and they did experience large declines during the tumultuous eighteen months. While it is not easy to view the losses on your statements, you realize you can be patient, because you do not need these assets for at least ten years. You stay calm and are very thankful to have other provisions for your shorter-term needs. The stock markets begin to slowly recover, and by early 2013 (fewer than six years from when the decline began), you have more than recovered your losses from these longer-term investments.

The ones who suffered the most during the down market of 2008–2009 invested funds needed in the near term too aggressively and were forced to withdraw them before the markets recovered. Or they panicked and sold everything to cash. You can afford to be patient when you invest according to your time frames.

Count the Cost

When I purchased the PolyMedica shares, I had no idea of the stress, distraction, and fear that was to follow. Even after losing almost all my profit, I was greatly relieved when I sold my shares. When we don't understand the risk, the time frame, or the stress that accompanies an investment, we set ourselves up for anxiety-filled days.

> The naive believes everything, but the sensible
> man considers his steps. (Prov. 14:15 NASB)

When you hear a sales pitch that promises a big investment return, make sure to count the cost. For example, it can be very enticing to purchase a rental property. The real estate agent explains land and property are tangible and hold their value well. Not only that, but the rental income should be sufficient to pay the mortgage and property taxes. And you can even use the property yourself for a few weeks during the year. Sounds great, doesn't it?

But have you counted the cost? What happens when the pipes burst in the middle of the night or the property needs a new roof? Are you prepared to pursue the tenant who is late with rent, or worse yet, one who does not pay at all and must be evicted? What if there is a long period of time when you can't find a renter? Are you prepared for the damage a careless renter leaves behind? While none of these considerations mean it is wrong to own rental property, it is a mistake to buy any investment without counting the costs.

Pursue Peace

Watch out for anxiety, because as Proverbs 12:25 says, "An anxious heart weighs a man down." Paul commands us in Philippians 4:6, "Be anxious for nothing," which includes our investments. Even when PolyMedica was at its height and the profits were substantial, I did not experience peace. The fact I excluded Susan from PolyMedica definitely multiplied my uneasiness. Prosperity is never a worthy substitute for peace.

Where to Invest

In addition to principles that guide our investment behavior, investors need to know where to invest. Investments perform best in countries that are growing and following sound economic principles. To determine which nations deserve our capital, we must analyze the characteristics of countries like we would evaluate companies.

Country Characteristics

- Income statements—revenue, growth projections, and government spending
- Balance sheets—deficits, debt levels, and fiscal policies
- Management—regulations, tax structure, and trade policies
- Workforce—demographics, birth rates, and productivity levels

An analysis of these distinctives uncovers those economies most likely to benefit from higher economic growth in the future. Don't be confused by short-term positive results in countries not reflecting sound economic policies. Over the long term, investment results will be highly correlated to their fundamental economic principles, good or bad. Wise investment counsel can help discern these factors in order to determine where to invest.

When to Invest

> There is an appointed time for everything. And there is a time for every event under heaven (Ecc. 3:1 NASB)

The timing of investment decisions is critical. Investments are often overpriced due to greed or undervalued because of fear. These misevaluations present both risks and opportunities. The future growth and inflation levels ultimately determine whether investments are purchased at reasonable prices. Current pricing can be tested by the economic growth and inflation expectations. Seek wise investment counsel to determine when to invest based on these factors.

Faithfulness

> Moreover, it is required of stewards that they be found trustworthy. (1 Cor. 4:2 ESV)

I am thankful for my PolyMedica experience. It will forever be a powerful reminder that faithful stewardship is about the process, not the result. While we often judge our decisions based on outcomes that are impossible to predict, God asks us to be faithful stewards, following a biblical process for making decisions. Then, free from anxiety and full of peace, we can leave the outcome in His competent hands.

Chapter 9

Who Needs a ~~Budget~~ Spending Plan?

U nclean water, lack of education, and corrupt governments are examples of third world problems. Americans have troubles my son Keaton calls "first world probs."

- I can only spray my lawn with clean, drinkable water on Mondays, Wednesdays, and Fridays.

- I can't find any movies I want to watch on Netflix.

- The chocolate chips in my milkshake are clogging my straw.

- It takes two connecting flights to get to St. Croix for the holidays.

- Rain caused water spots on my car's backup camera.

- My TV show did not record because the DVR is full.

- I am staying with relatives who don't know their Wi-Fi password.

- I forgot to back up my apps before updating my phone.

- My apple is too big for the apple slicer.

We are often distracted by these "problems," which hardly seem tragic when we realize they are not even a possibility for most of the world. We don't understand the world's poverty, and the world does not comprehend our wealth.

The Consumption Assumption

Most Americans place in the top 1 percent of the world's income, and we assume our abundance is for our enjoyment.[46] Andy Stanley calls this the "consumption assumption."[47]

Why has God given us so much? Is it just so we can be extra comfortable? If it is not all for our pleasure, how much should we spend?

The journey to determine how much we should spend begins with changing our assumption about consumption. A focus on spending money solely to acquire things causes us to live as if our time on earth is all that matters. This incorrect perspective distracts us from what matters most to God.

> Then He said to them, "Beware, and be on your guard against every form of greed; for not even when one has an abundance does his life consist of his possessions." (Luke 12:15 NASB)

Culture's popular plan is to pursue higher education in order to make more money so that we can buy more things, not remembering the danger that often accompanies our satisfaction with earthly comfort. One of the most frightening verses in Scripture highlights the peril of a life fixated on the temporal.

> As they had their pasture, they became satisfied, and being satisfied, their heart became proud; therefore they forgot Me. (Hos. 13:6 NASB)

Having an abundance makes it easy to become consumptive, which often leads to a migration of our hope from God to our riches. Is it any wonder history shows that when a nation's wealth increases, its collective dependence on God decreases?

> The poorest man I know is the man who has nothing but money. (John D. Rockefeller)

Where Is Our Focus?

It is our heart's focus, not our actual level of spending, which determines whether we love things and use people or love people and use things.

> Do not love the world, nor the things in the world. If anyone loves the world, the love of the Father is not in him. For all that is in the world, the lust of the flesh and the lust of the eyes and the boastful pride of life, is not from the Father, but is from the world. (1 John 2:15–16 NASB)

The Bible does not provide strict mandates explaining what amount of spending is consumptive and what is balanced. It is a matter of the heart whether our wealth is our treasure, regardless of how much we have.

> For where your treasure is, there your heart will be also. (Matt. 6:21 NASB)

A. W. Tozer provides four questions to help us discover our heart's treasure:

- What do we value most?
- What would we most hate to lose?

- What do our thoughts turn to most frequently when we are free to think what we will?

- What affords us the greatest pleasures?[48]

The realization that it is possible to spend too much allows us to grapple with the question of how much we should spend on living expenses. But before going any further in our budget making, we must deliberately ask the Lord to help us keep our gaze on Him, as King David prayed.

> One thing I have asked from the LORD, that I shall seek: that I may dwell in the house of the LORD all the days of my life, to behold the beauty of the LORD and to meditate in His temple. (Ps. 27:4 NASB)

How Much to Spend?

We determine our maximum spending level by following the priority order of spending, which begins by calculating how much we will need to cover charitable giving, taxes, debt payments, and saving for future needs. Once we subtract these from our income, the amount that remains establishes the *most* we can spend on living expenses without jeopardizing these higher priorities. We create financial stress when we spend our money backward—spending first on lifestyle and then hoping to have enough left for giving, taxes, debt, and savings.

Once we have calculated the maximum amount we can spend by following the priority order of spending, our second level of assessment is more difficult. Should we spend less than what we *could* spend? This is a personal decision that must not be legalistic but based on prayer and conversation with our spouse. The goal is to find a spending level that fights against the consumption assumption and protects our focus.

Give an Account

> So then each one of us will give an account of
> himself to God. (Rom. 14:12 NASB)

As a steward of God's resources, we should be able to give an account of our current spending. For many, just the thought of this type of recordkeeping creates anxiety. However, over the past few years, technological advances have reduced the amount of time needed to accurately track expenses and account balances.

The free and user-friendly web-based program Mint.com has set a new standard by making money management almost simple. Here is how it works. After establishing an account, add your various bank, credit card, and investment accounts by supplying Mint with your usernames and passwords. In this age of identity theft, this sounds risky. But Mint (an Intuit company) has gone to great lengths to be secure. By having read-only access to your financial accounts, Mint constantly updates your spending and balances.

The program automatically separates credit and debit card purchases into categories, which is a tremendous benefit. All your spending is made available to view through charts and graphs that enable you to assess your habits and patterns. Many other tracking systems exist, so find the one that helps you give an account.

Predetermine Spending

Our spending habits speak volumes about our priorities. When we review our patterns, we are more likely to make wise and God-honoring decisions about our future spending. This predetermining of expenses is usually called a budget. However, this "B" word has developed such a bad reputation, I prefer the kinder term "spending plan."

The goal of a spending plan is to help us spend money in

a way that is consistent with our priorities, protecting us from being consumptive and preventing our hope from drifting away from God and toward money. Begin by determining the overall amount you wish to spend. Remember, this cannot be more than what is left after giving, taxes, debt, and savings. And it may need to be an even lower number.

Once you determine the total amount necessary for living expenses, populate your individual categories. Start with fixed expenses and items that are not easily decreased. This includes categories such as insurance and utilities. Then move to the remaining categories that are most important to you. Keep in mind the goal is to not exceed your total amount for living expenses.

For example, we are in a phase of our lives where we spend a tremendous amount on food. We have three boys, one who is trying to gain enough weight to be a defensive end on his high school football team. So for us, it is important to spend more on food and less in some other areas.

No matter how much we earn, we all need limits, so we *all* need a spending plan and a good tracking system.

Invest in Relationships

Dr. Ken Boa, president of Reflections Ministries, once asked a powerful question: "If you had to summarize the Bible in one word, what would it be?"

There are many good responses, but Ken's insightful answer was "relationships." As he sees it, all Scripture points to the principal importance of our relationship with God and our relationship with each other. Jesus confirmed this value when He was asked to define the greatest commandment in Matthew 22:36–40. Christ answered, "You shall love the Lord your God with all your heart and with all your soul and with all your mind." And, "You shall love your neighbor as yourself."

Investing in our relationship with God and with people should be more consuming than our own comfort. If we create categories in our spending plan designated for investing in relationships, and if we create some margin in our budget to be able to respond to unexpected opportunities to bless others, we will experience authentic joy. By predetermining our spending, we can ensure resources are available for these purposes.

I have a passion to disciple high school boys. It began when Griffin was finishing up his eighth-grade year, and we decided to start a discipleship group with seven of his friends. The challenge was to create a study that was serious about teaching the Bible in a format that would make the guys want to keep coming back.

The plan was to gather every other Saturday night for several hours. Boys love to eat, so the evenings always began with a meal together, followed by the Bible study and some time to hang out. We based the format on Acts 2:42, which says, "They were continually devoting themselves to the apostle's teaching and fellowship, to the breaking of bread, and to prayer." The goal of the group was to become devoted followers of Christ.

As I spent more time with these young men, it became obvious my teaching needed to be more creative to impact them. So I began to incorporate games and video clips that related to the biblical topic we were studying. When we studied Revelation 3:16—where God says be hot or cold toward Him, not lukewarm lest He spit us out of His mouth—we had some fun to drive home the point. We held a contest to see who could keep an Alka Seltzer and a few ounces of Sprite in his mouth the longest. What ensued were eight boys trying to keep an erupting volcano in their mouths. Some had it coming out of their noses before relenting, but eventually they all were forced to spit it out. They loved the game, but more important, it made the point.

To this day, I can ask any of these young men, "Alka Seltzer and Sprite, what was the point?" Every one of them will tell me,

"Don't be lukewarm toward God!" We still have good laughs about that competition.

There was an investment of time and money involved in these interactive studies. I bought gifts for the guys for Christmas and graduation, and spent money on a projector, speakers, and a large portable screen on which to show PowerPoint slides and video clips. We were onto something, as the guys were growing in their relationship with God and one another. They were excited about the group, and they kept coming back.

I have done plenty of consuming in my life, and it can be enjoyable. But investing in people is much more satisfying, rewarding, and lasting. When we predetermine our spending and create a margin, we leave room for the things that are most important.

Chapter 10

Rethinking Retirement

In 1880, 78 percent of men over the age of sixty-five were still working. In 2012, despite a significant increase in the prior ten years, less than 24 percent of men aged sixty-five or older were still in the labor force.[49]

Clearly, something has changed regarding our view of retirement. It used to be assumed people would work their entire lives. Today, most would consider that a disaster. Somewhere along the way, the notion of being able to live comfortably without working became the primary goal. How did we get to the point where retirement grew to be so important that we start planning for it as soon as we begin our careers?

Retirement is an idea that was largely unknown just one hundred years ago. In the late 1880s, significant demographic changes began to alter the entire view of economic security. The Industrial Revolution moved the majority of workers from self-employed farmers to wage-earners. This was quite different from an agrarian society, whose labor provided food for the table.

Once income was primarily derived from wages, one's economic security was threatened by factors outside their control, such as layoffs and recessions.

In addition, the urbanization of America in the early 1900s led to the dispersion of the extended family. Until this time, multiple generations (including grandparents and other relatives) lived together. As one grew older, this offered the tremendous advantage of being cared for by family. Today, one of the reasons we work so hard to accumulate retirement funds is because we do not want to depend on children, who may be unwilling or unable to care for us.

By 1920, more people lived in cities than on farms for the first time in our history. At the same time, advances in health care enabled Americans to live longer than ever before, with the average life span increasing by ten years between 1900 and1930, the fastest increase in recorded history.[50]

These demographic changes were accompanied by a significant increase in income resulting from personal savings, employer benefits, a rising stock market, and government programs like Social Security and Medicare. Social Security was put into effect by FDR during the Great Depression for the purpose of freeing up jobs for the many unemployed young men in the country. Social Security retirement benefits were paid to those who were age sixty-five or older. At that time, the average life expectancy for a man was sixty-three. It was meant to be a short-term solution to a significant unemployment problem, not a widespread entitlement to entice millions to stop working while they were still able.

Rather than being pushed out of the marketplace due to obsolescence, most began to use their retirement benefits to facilitate an early exit from working. As a result, they started to long for something we would never have imagined years ago—being able to retire to a life of leisure while still healthy and active.

But, is this American dream of retirement all it is portrayed to be?

The Challenges of Retirement

A 2011 poll reveals that 25 percent of retirees think retirement is worse than working, and only 29 percent say leaving the workforce made life better.[51] Why does retirement often not deliver what is expected? The challenge of retirement is that unique struggles await our departure from the workplace.

Identity Crisis

After forty years of work, much of our self-image and identity are derived from our profession. This is especially true for those who have made a lot of money, as our worth is often linked to the fruits of our labor. When we no longer spend our days in a familiar place, the structure of life disappears. At the same time, we often encounter health issues that limit our activity. The combination of these factors can be overwhelming, especially when we no longer feel productive or useful.

This is similar to the struggle that moms face as their children grow older. After investing so much nurture and care in raising them, it is difficult to adjust to the reality that their grown children no longer need them in the same way they did when they were young.

As believers, our identity should always be based on who we are in Christ. More than ever, we must view ourselves through our Savior's eyes during these later years.

> But as many as received Him, to them He gave the right to become children of God, even to those who believe in His name, who were born, not of blood nor of the will of the flesh nor of the will of man, but of God. (John 1:12–13 NASB)

Fear of Not Having Enough

It is stressful to cover living expenses from savings rather than earned income. Regardless of how much we have, there is always a scenario that can deplete our assets—economic crisis, health issues, higher taxes, reductions in Social Security, severe inflation, or financial collapse. For this reason, financial peace of mind never results solely from how much we have.

The answer is found in prudently planning for the future, while making sure that our hope remains in God. Ultimately, He is the source of our provision. Remember, He owns it all, and we are just stewards. We cannot control the future, but we can control where we place our hope. Money is not worthy of our trust.

> Do not worry then, saying, "What will we eat?" or "What will we drink?" or "What will we wear for clothing?" For the Gentiles eagerly seek all these things; for your heavenly Father knows that you need all these things. But seek first His kingdom and His righteousness, and all these things will be added to you. Therefore do not be anxious for tomorrow; for tomorrow will care for itself. Each day has enough trouble of its own. (Matt. 6:31–34 NASB)

Spousal Adjustment

During our working years, we primarily see our spouses in the morning and at night. For many couples, it can be very stressful when, suddenly, they are together all day. While this is certainly not true for all in retirement, it is an issue for many.

Our office used to be located in midtown and was surrounded by many restaurants within walking distance. The easiest way to exit the building on the way to lunch was through the basement, past all the heating and air equipment. On several occasions, we noticed an older gentleman with a newspaper under his arm walking out a nondescript door next to the furnace room.

One day, overwhelmed by curiosity, we asked him what his business was. He replied, "Oh, I am retired." Noticing our confused looks, he continued. "I sold my business several years ago, but my wife wasn't used to having me around all day long. The owner of this building lets me have this little office for $200/ month. So I arrive around eight each morning, read the *Wall Street Journal,* and go home after lunch. It works well for both of us!"

We should not adjust to this transition by spending less time together but by making our marriage relationship a priority throughout our working years *and* in retirement. Don't wait until retirement to invest in each other. Pay more attention to your spouse's needs than to your own. Care for each other. Serve together. Find ways to be productive together. Pursue hobbies you both enjoy.

> Make my joy complete by being of the same mind, maintaining the same love, united in spirit, intent on one purpose. Do nothing from selfishness or empty conceit, but with humility of mind regard one another as more important than yourselves; do not merely look out for your own personal interests, but also for the interests of others. (Phil. 2:2–4 NASB)

The Problem with Traditional Retirement

The traditional idea of retirement assumes leisure provides more fulfillment than work. Stopping all paid employment and productivity to live a life of pleasure is actually not as enjoyable as we imagine. Remember God created us for work, and He values our labor over our leisure. While rest is critical as a means to refresh us so that we can continue to work, it is not a permanent goal to pursue.

> You shall work six days, but on the seventh day you shall rest; (Ex. 34:21a NASB)

Our golden years should be our most fruitful, since we have more time and money than ever before. A 2003 AARP study provides reasons why some decide to keep working past the age of sixty-five. The top three are the, "desire to stay mentally active, desire to stay physically active, and desire to remain productive or useful."[52]

When we realize the futility of a life focused on pleasure, we will not be in such a hurry to retire from being productive.

> I said to myself, "Come now, I will test you with pleasure to find out what is good." But that also proved to be meaningless. (Ecc. 2:1 NIV)

What Does Scripture Say about Retirement?

> This is what applies to the Levites: from twenty-five years old and upward they shall enter to perform service in the work of the tent of meeting. But at the age of fifty years they shall retire from service in the work and not work any more. (Num. 8:24–25 NASB)

This passage refers to the Levitical priests. It is the only verse in the Bible that mentions retirement. This rest of us function best by following God's work ordinance.

Work Ordinance

> Then the Lord God took the man and put him into the Garden of Eden to cultivate it and keep it. (Gen. 2:15 NASB)

As we discussed in chapter 4, even before sin entered the world, the earth had to be worked to fulfill its purpose, indicating our toil is part of God's perfect creation. Sin makes work hard, but labor is still necessary and good.

> For even when we were with you, we used to give
> you this order: if anyone is not willing to work,
> then he is not to eat, either. (2 Thess. 3:10 NASB)

We are given work to do because we are made in God's image, and He works.

> In his defense Jesus said to them, "My Father is
> always at His work to this very day, and I too am
> working." (John 5:17 NIV)

Work provides us with a wonderful opportunity to live out our faith. If we toil for the Lord, our labor is never in vain. Almost all work provides us with the opportunity to love God and to love and serve others.

> Therefore, my beloved brethren, be steadfast,
> immovable, always abounding in the work of the
> Lord, knowing that your toil is not in vain in the
> Lord. (1 Cor. 15:58 NASB)

In his book *Every Good Endeavor*, Tim Keller states, "We need to work for happiness." He goes on to say that work on this earth will be both frustrating and fulfilling. It will be frustrating due to sin and fulfilling because we are created to work. We cannot allow the frustration of work to cause us to quit being productive.[53]

Is Retirement Ever Appropriate?

To answer this question, we must remember how we defined work and determine an appropriate meaning for retirement. In chapter 4, we defined work as "the physical and mental energy exerted to be productive in what God has called and equipped us to do."

If we describe retirement as a life of ease and comfort and the complete absence of work, then it is not appropriate except for those who are unable to work. A better definition of retirement is, "a time in life when we have greater flexibility in how we are productive for God, since the need for earned income is greatly reduced or no longer needed."

When to Retire

Clients and friends often ask me, "When can I retire?" My typical response is, "You can retire whenever you want." The more important question is, "How long will your assets last at your current level of spending?" Since retirement means we will have less income, it is important to plan prudently.

> For which one of you, when he wants to build a tower, does not first sit down and calculate the cost, to see if he has enough to complete it (Luke 14:28 NASB)

This verse has great application for retirement planning. If we are going to reduce or eliminate income for the rest of our lives, we must count the cost so that we don't run out of money during the middle of our retirement. The two significant factors to consider are living expenses, which we can manage, and investment returns, which we cannot completely control. Using conservative investment assumptions, we must determine how much we can spend on an annual basis to protect our long-term goals.

Even when our financial projections indicate we will never run out of money, we must seek balance to make sure we keep our hope and trust in God, rather than the uncertainty of riches.

> Instruct those who are rich in this present world not to be conceited or to fix their hope in the uncertainty of riches ... (1 Tim. 6:17a NASB)

The ultimate goal is not wealth beyond measure, because the aim of a steward is to be faithful not rich. Counting the cost of retirement and being willing to control living expenses are parts of the process of being faithful. It is not enough, however, for the decision of retirement to depend only on a financial calculation. Too many people simply retire when they no longer need earned income. While this may be appropriate for some, the decision requires deeper analysis.

Should I Retire?

This is a far different question than, "Can I retire?" For some, the way they are most productive for the Lord is to keep working in their current vocations. I know Christians whose jobs give them incredible opportunities for influence, but their occupations come with great stress. For these, when the need for income is less, the answer may be to exchange stress for greater productivity and influence in an area of interest and passion.

What Am I Going to Do If I Retire?

This is critical to determine *before* retiring. Regardless of financial situation, if people do not know what they are going to do, they should not retire. And if the answer to this question does not involve being productive, further analysis is needed to avoid the emptiness that follows many retirees.

Some find retirement the perfect time to pursue their dream job or to follow their lifelong passion. Much of our lives are spent with the necessity of making a living, which can limit our working options and reduce our desire to take vocational risks. Retirement offers us the opportunity to spend time on what matters the most and to take risks that might not have been as practical early in our careers.

To help determine our passion, we can ask ourselves, "If I had no need to earn money, what would I do?" Regardless of whether we are near retirement or not, it may be worth pursuing our passion through our work, even if it means less money. Very few people regret following their passion, while many regret allowing money to be a primary motivator for their careers. The answers are varied and numerous, but too few ask the question.

Since deciding what to do in retirement is not always a simple process, it may be appropriate to slowly retire by reducing hours and taking time to explore other options for remaining productive. Look for opportunities to work less but to still work through flex time, telecommuting, job sharing, part-time work, or self-employment. Look for service opportunities. Books such as *Halftime* by Bob Buford or *The Second Half* by Lloyd Reeb have inspired many to develop a vision and create a plan to remain significant during the second half of life.

We can avoid the possible frustrations of retirement when we use the gifts and skills God gave us to serve others. Retirement is the perfect time to live according to our priorities and our passions, and to invest in relationships with our spouse, children, grandchildren, and others. This is the time to extend and expand our legacy and to share the wisdom that has been gained over many years.

> Gray hair is a crown of splendor; it is attained in the way of righteousness. (Prov. 16:31 NIV)

> Wisdom is with aged men, with long life is understanding. (Job 12:12 NASB)

Why Plan for Retirement?

If retirement is so often misinterpreted and overvalued, why should we bother planning for it? Because savings is a means of not presuming on the future. None of us knows how long we are going to be able to work. With life expectancies continuing to increase, it is logical to assume we will need to provide for ourselves for many years beyond what we are able to work.

> Go to the ant, O sluggard, Observe her ways and be wise, which, having no chief, Officer or ruler, Prepares her food in the summer, and gathers her provision in the harvest. (Prov. 6:6–8 NASB)

> There is precious treasure and oil in the dwelling of the wise, but a foolish man swallows it up. (Prov. 21:20 NASB)

The Balance of Saving

As we discussed in chapter 8, there are three ways to save: not enough, too much, or a prudent amount. The temptation for many in planning for retirement is to save too much, which the Bible calls hoarding.

> And he said, "This is what I will do: I will tear down my barns and build larger ones, and there I will store all my grain and my goods. And I will say to my soul, Soul, you have many goods laid up for many years to come; take your ease, eat, drink and be merry." But God said to him, "You fool! This very night your soul is required of you; and now who will own what you have prepared?" So is the man who lays up treasure for himself, and is not rich toward God. (Luke 12:18–21 NASB)

Hoarding is an excessive accumulation of money and things for the primary purpose of our own comfort and provision. It seeks to limit our dependence on God or anyone else. To be balanced is to responsibly plan for the future, while continuing to trust in God's sovereignty. The difference lies in where our ultimate hope is found, in God or our riches.

Define the Line

How do we respond when we have more money than we need? Have we ever asked God why He has given us more than we require?

Defining the line is the process of determining how much is enough to meet our financial goals. This begins by believing it is possible to have enough. Contrary to what many think, having a finish line results in freedom and peace rather than fear. Even though the actual line may be different for each of us, answering, "How much is enough?" keeps our hope fixed on God rather than money.

Retiring Well: Evans's Story

My friend, Evans, is a living example of retiring well. He shares his story below.

I was fifty years old, and my company was not for sale. Except for a two-year stint in the mortgage banking business after graduating college, the twenty-six years with this specialty construction business represented all I knew as a vocation. I had never given as much as a thought to selling my company, when I was approached with an offer from a current employee. My first consideration in contemplating a sale was, *What would I do with the rest of my life?*

Rather than instantly dismissing the offer, I decided to think and pray about it. For the first time in my life, I realized work had become an addiction to me. My motto was, "Find something you love to do, and you will never work a day in your life." While not all days were good, I really loved what I was doing. Being a highly specialized company with a lack of trained personnel, I was deeply involved in every detail. Somewhere along the way, though, the business started running me, and that concerned me.

As I reflected further, I longed for the day when life was not so dependent on the weather, a constant frustration in the construction business. And the substantial travel was beginning to wear on me.

Having two sons, I assumed my business would transfer the American way, to the next generation, despite the fact neither had expressed interest in my company. The reality is that they saw the long hours, the travel, an open briefcase on most nights, and the around-the-clock phone calls. Even though I loved what I was doing, frustration got the best of me too many evenings around the dinner table, when my battle cry was, "There has got to be a better way to make a living!" Lesson learned: be careful what you say! I believe I convinced them. It became clear that my boys were better off pursuing their own dreams, and I had to accept the fact the family business would not stay in the family.

After much prayer and deliberation, I made the decision to sell. The new owner asked me to stay with the company as a salesman and gave me the freedom to work as I saw fit. As we made the transition, I started to slowly pull away from my workaholic tendencies. I now look back with great thankfulness that I was able to gradually reduce my pace. I can't imagine how hard it would be to get the gold watch at the retirement party, clean out the desk, and have nothing to do the next day. That might be good for some, but not for me.

I had read about many business owners who retired early and quickly got bored. It seemed they either started a new business or died not too long after their initial retirement. Neither of those appealed to me, so I set out to find a purpose for the rest of my life while I still had the luxury of working. This question was my fork in the road. Would I use the rest of my life for my own pleasures or to have an impact for Christ? I chose the latter.

As my work slowed from the frantic pace of an owner, I started to use my free time in significant ways. This included volunteering for Crown Financial Ministries as a local contact, spending time with disadvantaged boys at the Boy's Farm in Newberry, South Carolina, and serving on a two-man construction team that oversaw an addition of a large worship center at my church.

When I was asked a few years later to take on a larger role with Crown, I sought counsel from several Christian friends, one of whom was my pastor. Knowing I was willing to volunteer my time, and knowing Crown was not the fit I had hoped it would be, he suggested I consider becoming the business administrator at the church. Seeing how well this lined up with my spiritual gifts and skills, I accepted his invitation and continue to occupy this extremely rewarding and fulfilling job today. God has placed me in my sweet spot.

Something else very significant happened along my retirement journey. Four years after selling my business, I took my first mission trip, which seemed impossible to do as a business owner. This trip was one of the most powerful experiences of my life, and I was hooked. I have now been on eighteen overseas mission trips in the past ten years. I continue to help organize and lead several trips each year for my church, and I love it. The privilege of spreading the gospel, the good work that is done, and the personal growth that occurs through these trips is incredible.

I am so thankful to my wife, who has been my wonderful marriage partner for over forty-three years. It is not easy to absorb the news that your husband is selling his business and the source of the family's income at age fifty. She has always wanted what was best for me and was immediately supportive. It has been a joy to spend more time with her and our children and grandchildren. I have been freed up to spend more of my time on what matters most, and for that I will forever be thankful.

Perhaps I could have muddled through the financial aspects of selling my business on my own, but I needed help to go outside the box of finances to figure out how to be most productive for the Lord in retirement. As I look back, I see how the question of, *What am I going to do?*, was more critical than the financial aspect of retirement.

Make the Most of This Time

We have the most wisdom, time, and money later in life, so we need to fight the misconceptions of retirement by realizing work is more fulfilling than leisure, and being productive is integral to life.

CHAPTER 11

PROVISION FOR LIFE'S MOST DIFFICULT TIMES

E very day, people are diagnosed with terrible sicknesses, suffer from natural disasters, and fall victim to senseless tragedies. Sometimes, the scope of these catastrophes is too difficult to comprehend. On December 26, 2004, a massive tsunami killed nearly 250,000 in a matter of hours in Indonesia, Sri Lanka, and other countries surrounding the Indian Ocean. More recently, our country was stunned and horrified in December of 2012 as twenty children (twenty-six total fatalities) were gunned down at Sandy Hook Elementary School in Newtown, Connecticut.

Why is there so much pain and evil around us? If God is good, why is the world full of so much sickness, disaster, and death? As we begin a chapter on the financial implications of life's most difficult times, it makes sense to first try to understand why this world does not work as God intended.

In the beginning, when the earth was created, everything was perfect, working just the way that God designed and desired. There were no floods, hurricanes, or tornados; no sickness or death. God granted humans complete authority over the earth, and it worked flawlessly.

> Then God said, "Let us make man in Our image, according to Our likeness; and let them rule over the fish of the sea and over the birds of the sky and over the cattle and over all the earth, and over every creeping thing that creeps on the earth." God saw all that He had made, and behold, it was very good. And there was evening and there was morning, the sixth day. (Gen. 1:26, 31 NASB)

So what went wrong? Sin entered the world. God only had one rule for Adam and Eve, that they not eat from the fruit of one particular tree.

Why did God have this rule? Because He knew we would gain something we did not want, the knowledge of good and evil.

> For God knows that in the day you eat from it your eyes will be opened, and you will be like God, knowing good and evil. Then the Lord God said, "Behold, the man has become like one of Us, knowing good and evil:" (Gen. 3:5, 22a NASB)

Until Adam and Eve sinned, there was no concept of evil. Everything was good. But their sin left a gaping chasm between how things should be and how they were. As a result, tragedies like the tsunami and the Newtown shooting happen, proof God's perfectly designed world has gone awry.

> Then to Adam He said, "Because you have listened to the voice of your wife, and have eaten from the

tree about which I commanded you, 'You shall not eat of it'; cursed is the ground because of you; in toil you will eat of it all the days of your life." (Gen. 3:17 NASB)

It is because of sin that God casts judgment on everything, and death enters our reality; everyone and everything must now die.

By the sweat of your face you will eat bread, till you return to the ground, because from it you were taken; for you are dust, and to dust you shall return. (Gen. 3:19 NASB)

God judges severely because He is perfectly just. This is not easy to understand. When we question how God can allow evil to exist, we fail to comprehend two things: how bad sin is and how good God is. We must hate our sin, for it is our collective sin that brings about pain, disaster, and death.

However, it is because of God's vast mercy that there is a solution. Through His Son, Jesus, He fixed the problem we created. We still face the consequences of sin on this earth, but God has a sinless world waiting for those who believe and place their trust in Jesus Christ. As we are surrounded by so much pain and suffering, our response should be, "Lord, forgive me for my sin which causes the evil in this world. For what I deserve is the full consequence of my sin, immediate and permanent separation from you. But, thank you, Lord, for your grace."[54]

For we know that the whole creation groans and suffers the pains of childbirth until now. And not only this, but also we ourselves, having the first fruits of the Spirit, even we ourselves groan within ourselves, waiting eagerly for our adoption as sons, the redemption of our body. (Rom. 8:22–23 NASB)

It is because of a fallen world and the consequences of sin that we need to discuss the need for insurance. Death, disability, and loss of property will occur. How should Christians prepare for and respond to these most difficult times from a financial perspective?

Insurance Overview

Being insured involves paying small premiums to avoid large losses. Insurance works because many people make payments to a company, who distributes funds to the few who suffer covered events. Actuaries ensure companies take in more premiums than they pay out in claims. Insurance is one of the primary ways we protect ourselves financially in the event of death, disability, and other disasters.

On the surface, it may seem those who have numerous claims benefit the most financially. In reality, this is not true. Nobody gets to the end of his or her life and says, "I can't believe I never got to use my homeowner's insurance policy, because my house did not burn down." We hope we never have to use our insurance coverage, but we have it to guard us from what could happen. This protection adds to our financial peace of mind.

While having some insurance is usually prudent for everyone, it is not possible or practical to insure against all loss. Our dependence must always be on God, not any financial plans we have made. The challenge is to determine where insurance is wise and where it is an attempt to avoid trusting God.

Since insurance in its current form did not exist during biblical times, it is not specifically addressed in Scripture. However, there are biblical principles and some practical thinking that can help guide our insurance decisions.

Biblical Principles Regarding Insurance

Protect and Provide

> The prudent see danger and take refuge, but the simple keep going and pay the penalty. (Prov. 22:3 NIV)

> Anyone who does not provide for their relatives, and especially for their own household, has denied the faith and is worse than an unbeliever. (1 Tim. 5:8 NIV)

As believers, it is wise to seek protection from danger and to provide for our families. We accomplish these, in part, through various forms of insurance.

Abide by Laws

> Let everyone be subject to the governing authorities, for there is no authority except that which God has established. The authorities that exist have been established by God. Consequently, whoever rebels against the authority is rebelling against what God has instituted, and those who do so will bring judgment on themselves. (Rom. 13:1, 2 NIV)

Laws and stipulations may require that we carry certain types of insurance. For example, most states mandate automobile liability insurance if we drive a vehicle, and mortgage companies necessitate property insurance for homes with a loan.

Choose Prudently

> Do not boast about tomorrow, for you do not know what a day may bring forth. (Prov. 27:1 NASB)

We should have enough so as to not presume upon God, but not so much that we stop trusting Him.

Do not worry then, saying, "What will we eat?" or "What will we drink?" or "What will we wear for clothing?" For the Gentiles eagerly seek all these things; for your heavenly Father knows that you need all these things. But seek His kingdom and His righteousness, and all these things will be added to you. So do not worry about tomorrow; for tomorrow will care for itself. Each day has enough trouble of its own. (Matt. 6:31–34 NASB)

Practical Thinking Regarding Insurance

Life-Stage Matters

What is a prudent amount of insurance? This is an individual decision based on budget, family needs, and stage of life. Those with young children and multiple financial needs often need more insurance. As net worth grows, we become increasingly self-insured and typically need less insurance. Similar to what we discussed with investments, it is not wise to have too little or too much insurance. Work with a life insurance agent or a financial planner to determine your specific needs.

Consider High Deductibles

Think of insurance as protecting against the catastrophic not the ordinary. This means it is often wise to use high deductibles and self-insure smaller risks when an adequate emergency fund is in place. Automobile, property, and health insurance are prime examples where this strategy can make sense.

Know the Company

When purchasing insurance, be sure to research the financial strength of the company through rating agencies like A. M. Best, Standard & Poor's, and Moody's.

Life Insurance

In general, life insurance should be viewed as a living expense, not as an investment, as it serves two primary purposes—survivor's benefits and estate liquidity.

Determining which type of life insurance to buy can be overwhelming, as information and opinions are numerous and varied. Two primary types of life insurance exist, term and permanent. Term has no cash value and is best suited for those whose life insurance needs do not carry into their later years. Permanent, including whole life, builds up cash value over time and is a good fit for those who will likely need life insurance forever, or at least until age sixty-five or seventy. Permanent premiums are much more expensive than term in the early years. But permanent can be the better value if insurance is needed for one's entire lifetime. When comparing the products that can meet your needs, it is essential to understand what you are buying.

> O LORD, my heart is not proud, nor my eyes haughty; nor do I involve myself in great matters, or in things too difficult for me. (Ps. 131:1 NASB)

Disability Insurance

Most of us are aware that we need life insurance. But we don't think as much about disability insurance. This is a bit surprising, since we are much more likely to become disabled than to die if we are younger than sixty-five.[55]

Disability insurance is designed to replace a portion of earned income if sickness or injury makes working impossible. This coverage is more important early in a working career, when a long-term disability could eliminate many years of income. It is not as critical as one approaches retirement, since most disability policies only pay benefits until age sixty-five or seventy.

Many employers provide group disability insurance, but this

is not always sufficient. Company policies usually cover 50 to 60 percent of one's current income, and the benefits paid are often taxable. If you are self-employed or if your group disability is not sufficient, consider purchasing an individual disability policy that fits into your budget. Don't count on Social Security Disability (SSDI) to provide for you, as the standards to qualify are stringent.

The goal of disability income should not be to avoid all work simply because you are not able to perform your current job. For example, a surgeon may no longer be able to operate with a hand that is permanently injured in an accident. But the doctor is still capable of teaching at a college or performing medical research. This is consistent with biblical wisdom found in 2 Thessalonians 3:10, which says, "If anyone is not willing to work, let him not eat." Look to disability insurance to provide protection for long-term permanent disabilities and to help bridge the gap for injuries and illnesses that decrease the level at which you are able to work.

Umbrella Liability Insurance

Virtually every state has laws that hold drivers financially accountable for bodily injury and property damage resulting from an accident. Similar laws exist for homeowners and watercraft owners. While most states require some level of liability insurance for automobile operators, those with significant assets may be wise to carry much higher levels of protection.

Umbrella liability insurance provides coverage beyond the limits of automobile and homeowner policies and is relatively inexpensive. Unlike some of the other insurance types we have discussed, the need for umbrella liability insurance protection actually increases as one's net worth grows. Check with your current insurer to inquire about the possibility of obtaining this type of policy.

Long-Term Care Insurance

Among the most significant financial threats we face late in life are the costs associated with long-term care. Seventy percent of those who are sixty-five or older will require some type of long-term care services during their lifetime, with the average need lasting three years. A staggering 20 percent will need care for more than five years.[56]

Depending on the type of services, current costs for long-term care range from $41,756 to $83,950 per year. For those who need care for several years, total costs can easily eclipse $250,000.[57]

Most of us should not count on the government to help cover these expenses. Medicare does not always pay for long-term care. When it does, it only covers the first twenty days and part of the next eighty days. Medicaid only provides coverage for long-term care for those with minimal incomes and few assets.

One way to reduce this significant risk is to purchase long-term care insurance. These policies pay a benefit to those who cannot accomplish several "activities of daily living" without assistance. These activities include eating, dressing, and bathing. After a waiting period, a monthly benefit is paid based on the terms of the policy and the expenses incurred. While the premiums are expensive, they can help offset much greater costs later in life. In most cases, the receipt of nine months of long-term care benefits is enough to equal or exceed the amount paid for all of the years of premiums.

Long-term care premiums are based on age and health at the time of purchase. Unlike many other types of insurance, these premiums do not increase every year. In fact, these policies used to be sold under the assumption premiums would stay consistent forever. But as Americans have been living longer and needing more long-term care services than originally predicted, almost all companies have been forced to increase premiums for both new and existing policyholders every few years. While there is not one ideal age to purchase long-term care insurance, it generally makes sense to consider doing so in your mid-fifties to early sixties.

Not everyone should purchase long-term care insurance. Some cannot afford the premiums or may determine the size of their assets do not necessitate having this type of coverage. Those with a larger net worth may be able and willing to self-insure. According to the Society of Actuaries, at least $2 million in investable assets is needed to be adequately self-insured for long-term care. Even at this level, other factors—such as lifestyle, dependents, and estate goals—must be considered before making the decision to purchase coverage or to self-insure.[58]

You can be creative with long-term care insurance. It is possible to lower premium costs by extending the waiting period and/or decreasing the monthly benefit. Even a partial policy can help offset some of the potential future costs.

When evaluating a long-term care insurance policy, consider these key components. First, only purchase a policy from a top-rated company that receives much of its revenue from products other than long-term care. This helps lessen the risk associated with trying to predict how many people will need extended long-term care in the future.

Second, most need to have a compound inflation rider that insures benefits will increase as medical costs rise. Last, it is wise to consider a home-health-care rider that allows benefits to be paid even if care is given at home, which is often the best situation.

This leads us to an important concern regarding long-term care insurance. In the past, the aged were valued for their wisdom, morality, and knowledge. Today, it is too common for the elderly to be viewed as a burden. As a result, nursing homes and retirement facilities are full of the neglected and the lonely. The truth is that the growing prevalence of long-term care insurance and a wide array of retirement facilities have made it much easier for us to push the care of our elders to others. This does not reconcile with the biblical mandate to honor our parents.

> Honor your father and mother (which is the first commandment with a promise), so that it may be well with you, and that you may live long on the earth. (Eph. 6:2–3 NASB)

A home-health-care provision is important because it provides the option for parents to live with children while they receive care. Don't get me wrong. There are times when a facility is the only way for someone to get the assistance they need. But far too many who are put in facilities live out their final years in deep loneliness, as their families are too busy to care for them.

Look Ahead

> Therefore we do not lose heart, but though our outer man is decaying, yet our inner man is being renewed day by day. For momentary, light affliction is producing for us an eternal weight of glory far beyond all comparison, while we look not at the things which are seen, but at the things which are not seen; for the things which are seen are temporal, but the things which are not seen are eternal. (2 Cor. 4:16–18 NASB)

> Then I saw a new heaven and a new earth; for the first heaven and the first earth passed away, and there is no longer any sea … and He will wipe away every tear from their eyes; and there will no longer be any death; there will no longer be any mourning, or crying, or pain; the first things have passed away. (Rev. 21:1, 4 NASB)

What is the ideal? The ideal is a world without sin, where there is no death, disability, or disaster. We call this heaven.

The reality is that we live in a world full of sin. As we encounter the constant effects of sin, it should cause us to focus on and be thankful for spending eternity with God in heaven. Until we get there, we are wise to consider insurance as a means to protect and provide for ourselves and our families, while making sure our hope and security remains in God.

Chapter 12

A Legacy Worth Leaving

O n a cold January morning, a thirty-nine-year-old man dressed in blue jeans and a baseball cap arrived at a Washington, DC Metro subway station and began to play the violin. For forty-three minutes, he brilliantly played six classical pieces for the 1,097 people who passed by, most of them on their way to work.

After sixty-three travelers scurried by without even a glance at the violinist, a middle-aged man slowed his pace for a couple seconds, looked in the direction of the music, and then hurried off to his destination. Thirty seconds later, a woman dropped a donation into his case, barely breaking her stride. It was six minutes into the performance before anyone stopped to listen.

For the entire time he played, only seven people stopped and listened for at least one minute. He received a total of $32.17 from twenty-seven people who mostly continued at a hurried pace after making their contributions. At the conclusion of each of the six pieces, no one applauded. For most of the time he was at the station, he went unnoticed, even though hundreds of commuters passed within several feet of him. It was if he were not there. Throughout the day, children instinctively wanted to stop and listen, but each time, a parent prodded them to move along; they had schedules to keep.

What the Metro station patrons didn't know was that the violinist was Joshua Bell, one of the most talented musicians in the entire world. He had perfectly performed several of the most complicated pieces ever written, and he did it on a three-hundred-year-old Stradivarius violin called the Gibson ex Huberman, worth $3.5 million!

Three days before his subway adventure, Bell sold out Symphony Hall in Boston, where most seats went for $100 or more. On this morning, he struggled to get people to listen to him for free.

Why was Bell performing in such an unusual venue? It was all part of a social experiment by the *Washington Post*. Would the passersby recognize and appreciate beauty and excellence in an unexpected time and place?

The greatest fear of those in charge was that Bell would be instantly recognized and a crowd would develop, blocking commuters from their destination. Despite playing a benefit at the Library of Congress the night before, only one person actually recognized Bell that morning. She stood ten feet away, front and center, and watched with great joy as hundreds slipped past her on both sides.

A few weeks later, Bell watched the video taken while he performed. He understood that people were on their way to work, so Bell was not surprised that he did not draw a crowd. What confounded him was that, despite the fact he was making an incredible amount of noise, he was invisible to most of the commuters. When several of the commuters were later told whom they had ignored, they had no excuse other than that were busy and had other things on their minds.[59]

If we do not have a moment to stop and listen to one of the best musicians in the world, playing some of the most beautiful music ever written, what else are we missing?

Andy Stanley teaches that we all need breathing room, space between our current pace and our limits. When we don't have enough margin, our stress level goes up, our focus narrows, and our relationships suffer. In other words, we neither notice nor take the time to hear the music.

Why do we allow this to happen?

Fear. The fear of missing out, of not having enough, or of falling behind. It can even be the fear of insignificance that pushes us to be so busy that we miss what matters the most.[60]

No one sets out to pursue riches over relationships, but many achieve this upside-down value. We are leaving the largest transfer of wealth in the history of the world to our children, but they are a generation who has not been prepared to handle it. We spend much of our lives creating riches and very little time imparting the discernment needed to manage it well. Is it possible that we could arrive at the end of our lives leaving more wealth than wisdom to our children and grandchildren? How do we cultivate a legacy worth leaving? The answers are right in front of us. We just have to take the time to see them!

The Beauty of Wisdom

> Wisdom along with an inheritance is good and an advantage to those who see the sun. For wisdom is protection just as money is protection, but the advantage of knowledge is that wisdom preserves the lives of its possessors. (Ecc. 7:11–12 NASB)

Since it is knowledge that makes an inheritance beneficial, we must figure out how to impart financial wisdom to our children and grandchildren so that they can be faithful stewards.

Training Children and Grandchildren

> You can't leave character in a trust account. You cannot write your values into the will. You cannot bank traits like courage, honesty, and compassion in a safe-deposit box. What we need is a plan—a long-term strategy to convey our convictions to the next generation. (Tim Kimmel)

> Train up a child in the way he should go, even when he is old he will not depart from it. (Prov. 22:6 NASB)

Seven Key Principles

It should come as no surprise that the key principles we need to teach our children and grandchildren to help them become faithful stewards also serve as a wonderful summary of what we have covered in this book. These principles are foundational and work at any income level.

Understand That God Owns It All

> The earth is the Lord's, and all it contains, the world, and those who dwell in it. (Ps. 24:1 NASB)

Almost everyone agrees with this intellectually, but too few put it into practice, as evidenced by the fact Christians and non-Christians look very similar financially. Ownership changes everything. When we are not the possessor, our responsibility is to manage what we have in the owner's best interest. It is from the Bible that we discover how God wants us to manage His assets.

Give Generously

> Instruct them to do good, to be rich in good works, to
> be generous and ready to share ... (1 Tim. 6:18 NASB)

Giving is what we are commanded to do first, consistently, and abundantly with our income. Giving reinforces that God owns it all and releases our grip on money and its grip on us. In a paradox that only the generous understand, there is more joy in giving than getting.

Set Long-Term Written Financial Goals

> Commit your works to the Lord and your plans
> will be established. The mind of man plans his way,
> but the Lord directs his steps. (Prov. 16:3, 9 NASB)

Since we are easily distracted in life, we need goals to provide direction and purpose. We should prayerfully set our goals, commit them to the Lord, and write them down.

Avoid the Excessive Use of Debt

> The rich rules over the poor, and the borrower
> becomes the lender's slave. (Prov. 22:7 NASB)

We have become far too comfortable with debt. From governments to families, excessive debt enslaves countries and individuals. Avoid it when possible, and work to eliminate it where it exists.

Avoid a Consumptive Lifestyle

> Then He said to them, "Beware, and be on your
> guard against every form of greed; for not even
> when one has an abundance does his life consist
> of his possessions. (Luke 12:15 NASB)

A life centered on things is a tremendous interference to a person's relationship with God. The Bible does not mandate one standard of living that is right for everyone. But it is clear our focus should never be on things. Avoiding a consumptive lifestyle always begins with spending less than we earn.

Build Liquidity

> Go to the ant, O sluggard, observe her ways and be wise, which, having no chief, officer or ruler, prepares her food in summer and gathers her provision in the harvest. (Prov. 6:6–8 NASB)

A prudent level of savings preserves peace of mind and helps us prepare for unanticipated expenses. This is also a sensible prerequisite before investing to meet longer-term goals.

Diversify

> Divide your portion to seven, or even eight, for you do not know what misfortune may occur on the earth. (Ecc. 11:2 NASB)

What great advice! Wealth might be created by being concentrated, but it is best preserved by being diversified.

Financial Disciplines

Try these activities to develop the financial disciplines children and grandchildren need to be faithful stewards.

Activities That Promote Giving

- Create a giving jar, where children contribute and then give away the first 10 percent of any money they receive.
- Open a NCF donor-advised fund in your children's names,

and make birthday or Christmas contributions they can donate to qualified charities.

Activities That Promote Smart Spending

- Offer children the choice of $5 now or $7 in two weeks to teach them delayed gratification.

- Take children to a junkyard or to a third world country to provide a different perspective.

Activities That Promote Saving

- Create a savings jar, and have your children place at least 10 percent of any money they receive in it.

- At the end of the year, match the amount saved (similar to a 401k).

Activities that promote planning

- Allow children to help plan a vacation with the task of staying within a predetermined budget.

- Give older children a larger allowance, with which they are responsible to cover their clothing and entertainment for the year. Help them to set up a Mint.com account to track their spending.

Activities That Promote Investing

- Open a discount brokerage account for your children and fund it with money they can use to purchase one or two stocks in which they have an interest.

- Track the stocks and help the children understand why the prices move up or down.

Creative Incentives

- Offer your kids $250 (or maybe even $500) if they read or listen to the entire Bible within two years. Explain that the purpose is to create a habit and love of reading God's Word. The motivation of money is just to help them stay on track.

- Create a list of "for hire" tasks around the house that you are willing to pay them to complete. These should be different from chores that are not compensated because they are part of family responsibility.

Estate Decisions

Prudent estate planning should consist of these five key decisions.

Decision One: How Much Should I Give to Children?

> A good man leaves an inheritance to his children's children. (Prov. 13:22a NASB)

Not Too Much

The Bible speaks positively about leaving an inheritance, especially in the Old Testament. However, biblical inheritances typically consisted of land or animals, things that had to be worked and maintained in order to provide income. Most gifts today consist of liquid assets, which often tempt recipients to reduce or eliminate their productivity.

> When there is a man who has labored with wisdom, knowledge and skill, then he gives his legacy to one who has not labored with them. This too is vanity and a great evil. (Ecc. 2:21 NASB)

Be cautious when choosing the amount to leave children. Too much left to children can demotivate them from being productive.

> It is good for a man that he should bear the yoke in
> his youth. (Lam. 3:27 NASB)

The value of your estate is often larger than you think, since it includes life insurance, retirement plans, and all your other assets. Many default to leaving the most money possible to their children. But the amount you leave should not exceed what your children can handle well.

> The almighty dollar bequeathed to a child is an almighty curse. No man has the right to handicap his son with such a burden as great wealth. He must face this question squarely; will my fortune be safe with my boy and will my boy be safe with my fortune? (Andrew Carnegie)

Think about these questions:

- What is the worst thing that can happen if I leave my children too much?
- What is the worst thing that can happen if I don't leave my children enough?
- What is the right amount to leave to my children?

Plan for Now

Determine how much you would leave to your children through your estate today. Don't get caught up in thinking about ten or twenty years from now. Estate planning must be done in the present, as changes can always be made to your documents in the future.

Should Children Always Be Left Equal Amounts?

The Old Testament custom was to leave a double portion to the oldest son.

But he shall acknowledge the firstborn, the son of
the unloved, by giving him a double portion of all
that he has, for he is the beginning of his strength;
to him belongs the right of the first-born. (Deut.
21:17 NASB)

Jesus was unsympathetic regarding fairness when talking to
a son whose brother received a larger inheritance.

And someone in the crowd said to Him, "Teacher,
tell my brother to divide the family inheritance
with me." But He said to him, "Man, who appointed
Me a judge or arbitrator over you?" (Luke 12:13–
14 NASB)

The Bible does not command that gifts or inheritances must
be the same among children. This should provide you freedom to
leave unequal amounts where warranted. If you choose to leave
equal gifts, consider giving all children the amount your least
responsible child can handle.

Decision Two: How Much Should I Give to Charity?

Even those who have been faithful and generous givers during
their lifetimes usually don't include charitable gifts in their
estates. In fact, only one out of ten includes his or her church as
a beneficiary.[61]

It is at least worth considering leaving a portion of our estates
to charity, as this can be a wonderful legacy. If a donor-advised
fund like NCF is used for estate giving, children can have the
privilege of choosing which charities receive their dollars. It is a
wonderful way for them to experience the joy of giving.

If retirement assets (IRA, 401k, etc.) are left to children,
they have to pay taxes on the full amount, allowing them to
spend only the after-tax portion. Thus, retirement assets are best

donated through an estate, since qualified charities are not subject to income taxes, allowing them to use 100 percent of the gift. Funding charitable estate gifts with retirement assets is a very efficient use of estate distributions.

Decision Three: When Should I Give?

> An inheritance gained hurriedly at the beginning
> will not be blessed in the end. (Prov. 20:21 NASB)

Estate Giving

It is not always wise to leave an inheritance all at once, especially to younger adult children. Thankfully, there is a tremendous amount of flexibility in estate planning. Through the use of trusts, it is possible to spread distributions over many years after the death of both parents. For example, you might decide to have one-third of the inheritance dispensed when your child reaches age twenty-five, one-third at age thirty, and the remainder at age thirty-five. The trustee can be given the authority to make early distributions for emergencies and other legitimate needs.

Lifetime Giving

Those with larger estates should consider if some of their surplus can be given to their heirs and charity before death. This is valuable for several reasons. First, if our children stand to receive a significant inheritance, handling smaller amounts wisely will give them a better chance at managing the larger amounts well.

Second, it may be more helpful for adult children to receive an inheritance while they are younger than through your estate at death. Perhaps those earlier gifts could make it possible to provide a Christian education for grandchildren, help a son or daughter start a business, or put a needed addition onto their house.

The same is true with charitable giving. We should consider

doing more of our giving while we are living to help fulfill God's purposes. Great joy comes from being able to see how God uses our gifts.

Decision Four: What Tools Should I Use?

Answering the first three estate questions makes decision four much simpler. Part of our stewardship responsibility is determining how our assets should be dispersed on our deaths. Yet, according to a survey published in 2009, only 35 percent of adults have a will in place.[62]

Each individual state determines how to handle estates of those who die without a will. The state's will is likely much different from what we would desire. Even though it is an uncomfortable process, executing estate documents is an important part of stewardship.

In general, everyone should have the following documents in place: a will, a durable power of attorney, and a health-care proxy. A revocable or living trust may be beneficial for some. Large and complex estates may require more sophisticated planning. These carefully chosen tools are important to ensure we accomplish our goals while minimizing fees and taxes.

Once your documents are drafted and executed, realize it may be necessary to change ownership and/or beneficiaries of certain assets. For example, a revocable or living trust will be most effective for assets that are titled in the name of the trust before death occurs. In a similar manner, make sure the beneficiaries of your life insurance and retirement assets reflect your goals. It is the beneficiary designations, not your estate documents, which control the ultimate distribution of assets that have a beneficiary.

Decision Five: Do I Need a Family Conference?

For larger and more-complex estates, or for those who plan to give significant amounts to charity, it is wise to have a family conference where Mom and Dad can explain their logic and make sure intentions are known and understood. It is not always necessary to share the dollar amounts involved with the estate, as this can depend on the ages of the children and the ultimate goals you want to accomplish through the conference.

Everyone has a family conference shortly after death. But the reading of the will might be met with confusion, misunderstanding, hurt feelings, and even bitterness if this is the first time it has been discussed. Because money has the potential to harm relationships, a family conference while parents are living can be a wonderful tool to explain intentions while emotions are calm.

Financial Faithfulness

Just like the commuters who did not recognize the beauty of the violinist because they were busy and had other things on their minds, the distractions of money cause believers to often pass by the splendor, magnificence, and power of God's Word. Be the one who stops and listens to the Bible daily, while the rest of the world rushes by.

Cherish it.

Obey what it says.

Financial faithfulness is adopting a biblical perspective of money for ourselves and imparting this wisdom to our children and grandchildren. When it comes to developing a legacy worth leaving, don't miss the opportunities to grasp and impart the wisdom that preserves life!

EPILOGUE

I magine your family decides to take a summer car trip from the East Coast to California. For months you prepare, finding the best dates to avoid conflicts, determining where to stop and what to see, and making all the reservations. It's going to be the perfect vacation adventure! Finally, the day arrives to leave on your journey.

After carefully packing the car, you are ready to go. Your plan is to drive for seven hours and arrive in time for dinner reservations at a family-style restaurant several friends recommended. You'll stay the night at a nearby hotel.

You make the last-minute checks around the house to ensure the necessary lights are on and the appliances are off. After locking the doors, you head to the automobile, where your family waits with great anticipation. As you approach your car, you notice the tires don't look quite right. On closer inspection, you see the tires are bald. Hardly any tread is left on them! How could you have missed this? For weeks, your time and attention were devoted to planning every detail of this trip, yet somehow, you forgot to check the tires.

You know from experience it will take hours to get new

tires, especially on a Saturday without an appointment. You will certainly miss your dinner reservations, and the ordeal could even set the trip back an entire day. It will be almost impossible to rework the schedule. Not wanting to deal with the hassle, you decide to keep the information about the tires to yourself and take your chances. You figure that once you're in California, you will have time to buy new tires before your return trip home. With that as your plan, your vacation begins.

During your drive, you constantly worry about the tires. For the first two days of travel, the weather is good, and the car does fine. But on the third day, you encounter rain. While the rest of your family calmly sleeps in their seats, you are tense and jittery at the wheel. At one point, the car in front of you stops short, and you have to hit your brakes hard. Your car starts to skid, but the tires grab hold of the road just in time to prevent a rear-end collision. Your passengers stir and you assure them, "It's fine. Just avoiding a crazy driver in front of me."

When you finally arrive in beautiful California, you are so relieved. You made it! The next morning, you get four new tires put on your car. You don't even mind that it takes three hours. As you drive back to the hotel, you have peace of mind behind the wheel for the first time since leaving home.[63]

In many ways, this story reflects how we deal with money. We are tempted to determine financial success based solely on the outcome. If we end up with a lot of money, we feel successful. We don't take into account all the stress along the way and whether our decisions were wise or faithful.

That manner of handling money is similar to assuming it was a good decision to drive to California on bald tires, simply because you made it there safely. In reality, you subjected your family to unnecessary risk, and you were riddled with stress and anxiety.

Our financial journey matters to God. That is why Paul says in 1 Corinthians 4:2, "Moreover, it is required of stewards that they be found faithful." He does not say the goal of a steward is to end up with the most, because He is in charge of the results. When it comes to managing money, we must be consumed with discovering what is required to be faithful. This is how we live a life of financial faithfulness!

> His master said to him, "Well done, good and faithful slave. You were faithful with a few things, I will put you in charge of many things; enter into the joy of your master." (Matt. 25:21 NASB)

Xander and Blair afraid to leave the line to get the ball!

An example of the content children from the Dominican Republic.

Griffin's written goal to play baseball in college, "if it's God's will."

![Griffin at bat]

Griffin at bat for UAB against Rice.

Roger and Xander with our "one"—Evelyn!

Keaton may have been nervous in the batter's box, but he has no fear of flying!

This is the high school discipleship group in action.

The Gum family: Griffin, Susan, Keaton, Roger, and Xander.

MORE ONLINE

www.FinFaith.com

If you desire to further explore *Financial Faithfulness,* please visit *www.FinFaith.com,* where you can

- download study guides and leader's guides;
- watch a video of Roger talking about *Financial Faithfulness;*
- access free high school discipleship curriculum;
- contact Roger;
- and more!

Notes

1. This story occurred before HIPPA made it illegal for a medical professional to share this type of information.

2. Randy Alcorn, *Money, Possessions, and Eternity* (Wheaton, Ill.: Tyndale, 1989), 16, 17.

3. Quoted in a news report from the Barna Group, "Faith Has a Limited Effect on Most People's Behavior," May 24, 2004.

4. Quoted on *Bloomberg.com*, "For Millionaires 'Wealthy' is 7.5 Million, Fidelity Says," Elizabeth Ody, March 14, 2011. *www.bloomberg.com/news/2011-03-14/comfort-level-for-some-millionaires-is-7-5-million-fidelity-survey-says.html*.

5. From the Global Rich List, based on figures from the World Bank Development Research Group. *www.globalrichlist.com/*.

6. Randy Alcorn, *Money, Possessions, and Eternity* (Wheaton, Ill:Tyndale, 1989), 301.

7. Ben Patterson, *The Grand Essentials* (Waco, Tex.: Word, 1987), 17.

8. Quoted by Richard Halverson, *Perspective* (June 24, 1987).

9. Dacher Keltner, "Social Class as Culture: The Convergence of Resources and Rank in the Social Realm," *Current Directions in Psychological Science* (August 2011), 246-250.

10. Richard Watts, *Fables of Fortune: What Rich People Have that You Don't Want* (Austin, Tex.: Emerald Book Company, 2012),

11. Charles Haddon Spurgeon, "The New Park Street Pulpit Declension from First Love," sermon 217, delivered on Sabbath evening, September 26, 1858, by the Rev. C. H. Spurgeon at New Park Street Chapel, Southwark.

12. Randy Alcorn, *Money, Possessions, and Eternity* (Wheaton, Ill.: Tyndale, 1989), 119, 120.

13. Quoted by FDIC at *www.fdic.gov/about/comein/files/foreclosure_statistics.pdf.*

14. *www.issacharinitiative.org/.*

15. *www.lastlanguagescampaign.org/LLC.aspx.*

16. *www.billygraham.org/myhope_index.aspx.*

17. Author unknown.

18. .Adapted from Randy Alcorn, *Money, Possessions, and Eternity* (Wheaton, Ill.: Tyndale, 1989), 193, 194.

19. John Ortberg, *When the Game Is Over, It All Goes Back in the Box* (Grand Rapids, Mich.: Zondervan, 2008).

20. Spoken by Dr. Howard Hendricks at *KC 83* sponsored by Campus Crusade for Christ in Kansas City, MO December 31, 1983

21. Gail Matthews, "Study Backs Up Strategies for Achieving Goals" Dominican University, *www.dominican.edu/dominicannews/study-backs-up-strategies-for-achieving-goals.*

22. American Institute of CPAs, "AICPA Survey: Finances Causing Rifts for American Couples," May 4, 2012, *www.aicpa.org/press/pressreleases/2012/pages/finances-causing-rifts-for-american-couples.aspx.*

23. C. S. Lewis, *The Problem of Pain* (New York: HarperCollins, 1944/2001), 115.

24. Results published in the January 2010 issue of the journal *Personality and Individual Differences* of a study undertaken at Kansas State University by lead investigator James Daugherty, *www.k-tate.edu/media/newsreleases/dec09/gratification122409.html*

25. Dov Greenberg, "The Man Who Changed His Life After Reading His Obituary", *www.chabad.org/library/article_cdo/aid/271383/jewish/The-Man-who-Changed-his-Life.htm.*

26. Howard Dayton, *Your Money Counts* (Wheaton, Ill.: Tyndale House, 2011), 86.

27. Charles H. Spurgeon, *The Treasury of David Psalm 127* (Gaithersburg, Md.: Henderson Publishing, 1988).

28. Christian Smith, Michael Emerson, and Patricia Snell, *Passing The Plate: Why American Christians Don't Give Away More Money* (New York: Oxford University Press, 2008).

29. Jon Ronsvalle and Sylvia Ronsvalle, *The State of Church Giving through 2010* (Champaign, Ill: Empty Tomb, Inc., October 2012).

30. Research by The Barna Group in January 2008.

31. Don McClaren, *The Tithe as Teacher: An Energizing Force* (New York: The Office of Stewardship, The Episcopal Church Center, November 1980. Reproduced in winter 1982).

32. C. S. Lewis, *Mere Christianity* (San Francisco: Harper San Francisco, 1952/2001).

33. Andy Stanley, "One, Not Everyone." Sermon given at North Point Community Church, Alpharetta, Ga., January 2, 2011.

34. Brian Kluth, "2010 State of the Plate Surveys." *www.stateoftheplate.info/ Best-Financial-Advice-Bible-Reading-Leads-to-More-Giving-Less-Debt.htm.*

35. Kevin Duncan, "Americans Paying More in Taxes than for Food, Clothing, and Shelter." *www.taxfoundation.org/article/americans-paying-more-taxes-food-clothing-and-shelter* (May 3, 2012).

36. William McBride, Kyle Pomerleau, and Elizabeth Malm, "Tax Freedom Day." *Tax Foundation: taxfoundation.org/article/tax-freedom-day-2013-april-18-five-days-later-last-year* (April 2, 2013).

37. Tax Foundation, "U.S. Federal Individual Income Tax Rates History, 1862–2013 (Nominal and Inflation-Adjusted Brackets)", *http:// taxfoundation.org/article/us-federal-individual-income-tax-rates-history-1913-2013-nominal-and-inflation-adjusted-brackets.*

38. Max Lucado, "The Power of Election Prayer." *maxlucado.com/read/blog/ the-power-of-election-prayer/* (November 6, 2012).

39. Lewis Grizzard, "Trump's Fall Is Sad Testament to Debt Generation," *Atlanta Journal & Constitution* (June 24, 1998), excerpts only.

40. Richard Halverson, former Chaplain of the US Senate.

41. Steve Rhode, "Bankruptcy Filings Down in 2012, Continued Bad News for Debt Relief Industry," *Huffington Post,* November 7, 2012, *www.huffingtonpost.com/steve-rhode/bankruptcy-filings-down-i_b_2089617.html.*

42. Howard Dayton, *Your Money: Frustration or Freedom?* (Wheaton, Ill.: Tyndale House, 1979), 50.

43. Jeannine Aversa, "Stress over Debt Taking Toll on Health," *USA Today,* June 9, 2008.

44. *Guideposts,* 1999.

45. "Memorable Quotes for *Wall Street* (1987)." *Internet Movie Database: www.imdb.com/title/tt0094291/quotes.*

46. Annalyn Censky, "Americans Make Up Half of the World's 1%," *CNN Money: money.cnn.com/2012/01/04/news/economy/world_richest/index.htm* (January 4, 2012).

47. Andy Stanley, "Guardrails Part 5: The Consumption Assumption," sermon given at North Point Community Church, Alpharetta, Ga., May 16, 2010.

48. A. W. Tozer, "The Transmutation of Wealth," in *Born after Midnight* (Harrisburg, Pa.: Christian Publications, Inc., 1959), 106.

49. Moen, Jon R., "Essays on the Labor Force and Labor Force Participation Rates: The United States from 1860 through 1950," Ph.D. dissertation, University of Chicago, 1987; Dora L. Costa, *The Evolution of Retirement: An American Economic History, 1880–1990* (Chicago: University of Chicago Press, 1998); Bureau of Labor Statistics, *www.eh.net/encyclopedia/article/short.retirement.history.us.*

50. "Traditional Sources of Economic Security",*www.ssa.gov/history/briefhistory3.html.*

51. Jennifer Ludden, "Retirement: Reality not as Rosy as Expectations" (NPR, the Robert Wood Johnson Foundation, and the Harvard School of Public Health, September 27, 2011), *m.npr.org/news/front/140680583.*

52. Kathi Brown, "Staying Ahead of the Curve 2003: The AARP Working in Retirement Study," *http://www.aarp.org/work/working-after-retirement/info-2003/aresearch-import-417.html.*

53. Timothy Keller, *Every Good Endeavor* (New York: Dutton, 2012), 47.

54. Andy Stanley, "God Is Great, God Is Good: If So, Then Why" and

"All Things New," sermons given at North Point Community Church, Alpharetta, Ga., 2004.

55. Statistical information derived from the Society of Actuaries, the National Safety Council, the Million Dollar Round Table, the National Underwriter—May 2002, the JHA Disability Fact Book—2003/2004 Edition—Need for Disability Insurance. *www. affordableinsuranceprotection.com/death_vs_disability.*

56. "How Much Care Will You Need?", National Clearinghouse for Long Term Care Information, *longtermcare.gov/the-basics/ how-much-care-will-you-need/*

57. "Genworth 2013 Cost of Care Survey: Home Care Providers, Adult Day Health Care Facilities, Assisted Living Facilities and Nursing Homes", *www.genworth.com/dam/Americas/US/PDFs/Consumer/ corporate/131168_031813_Executive%20Summary.pdf.*

58. Society of Actuaries, "Segmenting the Middle Market: Retirement Risks and Solutions Phase II Report", *www.soa.org/research/research-projects/pension/research-segmenting-market-phase-2.aspx.*

59. Gene Weingarten, "Pearls Before Breakfast", *Washington Post* (April 8, 2007), *www.washingtonpost.com/wpdyn/content/article/2007/04/04/ AR2007040401721.html* (watch a video of this on YouTube by searching for "Joshua Bell You Tube .Washington Post").

60. Andy Stanley, "Breathing Room: Ex-Squeeze Yourself," sermon given at North Point Community Church, Alpharetta, Ga., January 6, 2013.

61. George Barna, *How to Increase Giving in Your Church* (Ventura, Calif.: Ventura, 1996), 33.

62. Harris Interactive, "Lawyers.com Survey Reveals Drop in Estate Planning by Americans in 2009; Ailing Economy Likely Reason." *Lawyers.com* (February 25, 2010), *press-room.lawyers.com/2010-Will-Survey-Press-Release.html.*

63. This story is courtesy of Vince Birley, Ronald Blue & Co., Atlanta, Ga.

* The cost of living in Durham is the same for me as it is for a millionaire. To include for comparison purposes people who live below the ~~pout~~ poverty line and places where the cost of living is 'lower' does not offer a balanced perspective on who's wealthy and who's not.